THE VACUUM PRINCIPLE

HOW TO FIND MARKET GAPS AND CREATE CATEGORY-DEFINING COMPANIES

Rajesh Srinivasan

Dedicated to those who see market gaps as opportunities,
Who fills those gaps with innovation,
And build tomorrow's industries from today's
overlooked market spaces.

Contents

**Part 3
The Cognitive Frameworks of
Market Creators**

Introduction: The Power of Empty Spaces

It was a rainy evening in Paris in 2008 when Travis Kalanick and Garrett Camp couldn't find a taxi. As they stood there, frustrated and wet, they weren't just experiencing a minor inconvenience— they were standing in a market vacuum.

But this isn't just a story about Uber. Every day, we walk past market vacuums – empty spaces of opportunity – without noticing them. Like gravity, these vacuums exert a constant pull on markets, waiting for someone to discover and fill them. And just like the physical universe abhors a vacuum, markets rush to fill these empty spaces with unstoppable force.

It was during a consulting project in Bangalore in 2019, I first began to crystallize this idea of market vacuums. I was working with a struggling food delivery company that was trying to compete with established players like Swiggy and Zomato. During a particularly frustrating strategy session, their founder looked at me and said, "We're trying so hard to be better, but maybe we're fighting the wrong battle entirely."

That comment struck me. Over cups of *masala chai* at a local cafe, we sketched out all the things food delivery companies weren't doing. Instead of focusing on what existed, we mapped the empty spaces – the vacuums. The company eventually found success not by competing in meal delivery, but by identifying and filling a completely different vacuum: connecting home chefs with bulk corporate catering opportunities. This wasn't just a pivot; it was a fundamentally different way of seeing the market.

This experience made me revisit dozens of cases I'd worked on over the years. I began to see a pattern – the most successful companies weren't just doing things better, they were finding and filling empty spaces that others hadn't even recognized existed.

I observed this phenomenon repeatedly while studying market patterns across geographies. In Mumbai, a street vendor noticed office workers couldn't get lunch delivered to their desks – a vacuum. He created a network of dabbawalas that now delivers 200,000 lunches daily. In Stockholm, a void in sustainable fashion led to the creation of H&M's Conscious Collection. In Lagos, the gap between traditional banking and modern needs gave birth to innovative mobile payment solutions. These weren't just lucky breaks or random successes – they were vacuums being filled.

The most successful businesses do more than fill existing market gaps—they actively create new opportunities. Apple redefined what a phone could be, not just addressing a market need but engineering an entirely new category. Netflix didn't simply meet a demand for entertainment; they revolutionized how people consume content by establishing new viewing habits. Similarly, Amazon went beyond spotting gaps in retail— they transformed the landscape by systematically innovating in convenience, selection, and speed.

This book isn't just about finding gaps in markets. It's about understanding the fundamental forces that create these gaps, learning to engineer them, and mastering the art of filling them at exactly the right moment. It's about seeing the invisible spaces where opportunity lives.

Over the last one year, my research team and I have delved deep into the principles of what I call "The Vacuum Principle." By analyzing hundreds of case studies, from the rise of Uber to the reinvention of the coffee shop experience by Starbucks, we've uncovered the fundamental patterns that allow companies to not just identify gaps but engineer entirely new spaces of opportunity.

In this book, you'll discover the five distinct types of market vacuums we've identified - feature vacuums, experience vacuums, price vacuums, access vacuums, and trust vacuums. Each one requires a unique approach, and understanding their characteristics will empower you to consistently spot the hidden potential that others so often overlook.

We'll explore the art of systematic vacuum spotting, equipping you with the tools to read market pressures, uncover customer frustrations, and map competitive blind spots. From there, we'll dive into the science of vacuum engineering, revealing how companies deliberately create new market spaces through meticulously architected value propositions, demand generation tactics, and psychological reframing.

Of course, vacuum creation is only half the battle. The other critical piece is market timing - understanding the three dimensions of market readiness that must align for successful vacuum filling. We'll examine how visionary companies like Amazon, Southwest Airlines, and Spotify timed their innovations perfectly, as well as strategies for defending your hard-won vacuums and scaling them into lasting competitive advantages.

Underlying this entire journey are seven distinctive mindsets that set apart the true vacuum creators - from intersectional curiosity to scale paradox mastery. These cognitive frameworks are the tools that allow them to see and seize opportunities that others simply can't.

Whether you're an entrepreneur searching for your next big idea, an executive seeking growth opportunities, or an investor hunting for the next market-defining innovation, understanding *The Vacuum Principle* will transform how you approach the world of business. It's the most powerful force I've encountered and mastering it will change how you look at markets, opportunities, and value creation forever.

Welcome to the world of *The Vacuum Principle*. Let's explore the power of empty spaces and unlock the hidden potential that so often goes unnoticed.

What is a Market Vacuum?

A market vacuum is an unmet need, an inefficiency, or a gap in the marketplace that exists between what currently exists and what could potentially solve a problem more effectively. Think of it like an empty space in an ecosystem waiting to be filled — a space where value could be created but hasn't been recognized or addressed yet.

Just as nature abhors a vacuum and instinctively works to fill it, markets exhibit a similar behavior—moving swiftly to address unmet needs and inefficiencies.

Understanding Market Vacuums

Chapter 1

Natural vs. Created Vacuums

In business, not all opportunities are created equal. Some emerge naturally from changing market conditions, while others must be deliberately engineered. Understanding this distinction - between natural and created vacuums - can mean the difference between catching a wave and creating an entirely new ocean.

As an acute observer of markets and innovation, I've always been fascinated by how opportunities emerge. Sometimes they appear like a river carving a new path – natural, inevitable, almost predictable if you know where to look. I think of these as nature's way of solving market inefficiencies. Other times, opportunities must be deliberately imagined and engineered, like architects designing spaces that never existed before. These created opportunities often seem obvious in hindsight, but they required someone to first imagine what could be.

The deeper I studied market-defining companies, the clearer this pattern became. Some found success by being first to spot and fill naturally emerging gaps. Others achieved greatness by creating entirely new spaces that nobody knew they needed. This chapter explores this crucial distinction and its implications for market creation.

The Art of Discovery and Design

In 1974, a church choir member and 3M scientist named Dr. Arthur Fry was frustrated during rehearsals. The paper bookmarks he used to mark pages in his hymnal kept falling out. This minor annoyance led him to think about an interesting possibility: what if there could be a bookmark that would stick to the page without damaging it?

Fry remembered an unusual adhesive that his colleague, Dr. Spencer Silver, had accidentally created in 1968 while attempting to develop a super-strong adhesive. Instead of creating a stronger glue, Silver had created something peculiar – an adhesive that was pressure-sensitive and could be reused. At the time, no one could figure out what to do with this solution without a problem.

This connection between Fry's bookmark problem and Silver's unusual adhesive would lead to the creation of Post-it Notes. But here's what makes this story fascinating: Fry and Silver didn't just identify a natural vacuum in the market – they helped create an entirely new one. Before Post-it Notes, people didn't know they needed repositionable paper. The market gap was engineered, not discovered.

The Dual Nature of Market Vacuums

Market vacuums manifest in two fundamental forms: natural and created. While both types represent opportunities for value creation, they demand distinctly different approaches, capabilities, and strategies. Understanding this crucial distinction enables organizations to craft appropriate strategies for each type of opportunity.

1) Natural Vacuums: The Power of Evolution

Natural vacuums emerge organically through the confluence of multiple market forces, technological advances, and shifting consumer behaviors. To understand how these forces combine to create opportunities, let's examine two contrasting examples of natural vacuum identification and exploitation - one from the last decade of retail transformation in India, and another from the revolution in urban mobility.

The Rise of Quick Commerce: A Vacuum Hiding in Plain Sight

When Albinder Dhindsa co-founded Grofers (now Blinkit) in 2013, he thought he was entering a well-understood market. India had several established players in the grocery delivery space, from BigBasket to Amazon Fresh. The natural vacuum seemed obvious - making grocery shopping more convenient for busy urban professionals.

But sometimes, the most profound market vacuums reveal themselves through unexpected events. In March 2020, as India entered its first pandemic lockdown, Dhindsa noticed something fascinating in their order data. Customers weren't just ordering larger baskets for planned weekly shopping. They were making frequent, small orders for immediate needs - a pattern that existing delivery models weren't designed to serve.

This observation led to a crucial insight: the real vacuum wasn't in planned grocery delivery. It was in the urgent, unplanned moments of daily life. The forgotten ingredient while cooking. The sudden need for medicine. The late-night snack craving. Traditional e-commerce was optimized for selection and price, but a massive vacuum existed in immediacy.

What made this vacuum particularly intriguing was how it had remained hidden despite being omnipresent. Traditional retailers saw delivery times as a constraint to be managed, not an opportunity to be exploited. Even existing quick-delivery services viewed 45-60 minutes as "fast enough." But Dhindsa and his team saw something different - they saw how rapid urbanization, changing consumer behaviors, and advancing technology had created the conditions for a new kind of retail.

In December 2021, Grofers rebranded to Blinkit with a radical promise: 10-minute delivery. This wasn't just a faster version of existing services. It was a fundamental reimagining of urban retail, requiring:

- A complete redesign of the supply chain with dark stores every 2 kilometers

- New inventory management systems optimized for immediacy rather than selection

- Novel rider allocation algorithms that could guarantee delivery times

- Reimagined store layouts focused on pick-and-pack speed

The most fascinating aspect wasn't just that Blinkit identified this vacuum - it was how they systematically filled it through innovation. Their 10-minute delivery promise didn't just meet an existing need; it created new consumer behaviors and expectations. As customers experienced the magic of instant delivery, they discovered needs they never knew they had.

The quick commerce revolution also reveals another crucial insight about vacuum creation: timing matters as much as identification. The same opportunity existed years earlier, but the confluence of digital payments, smartphone penetration, urban density, and changing consumer behaviors made 2021 the perfect moment for this innovation to take hold.

Natural vacuums emerge not through deliberate design, but through the organic confluence of market forces, technological shifts, and changing human behaviors. Take Blinkit's 10-minute delivery model: it wasn't invented out of thin air, but discovered in the unnoticed spaces between traditional grocery delivery and urban consumer needs. The pandemic, smartphone penetration, and shifting lifestyles created a silent opportunity that existed long before anyone recognized it. The art lies in recognizing these nascent possibilities before they become obvious to everyone.

Blinkit's journey illuminates the essence of natural vacuums: they are not manufactured but discovered. Hidden in the everyday friction of urban life, these opportunities emerge when market forces, technological advances, and changing behaviors converge. The 10-minute delivery wasn't just an innovation—it was the natural evolution of retail, waiting to be understood. The true insight lies not in creating something new, but in perceiving the unmet needs that have always existed, just beyond our immediate view.

2) Created Vacuums: The Art of Engineering Opportunity

In stark contrast to natural vacuums, created vacuums emerge through deliberate engineering of new market spaces. Tesla's approach to electric vehicles provides a master class in vacuum creation. While there was a natural vacuum in sustainable transportation, Tesla chose to engineer an entirely different vacuum: high-performance, luxury electric vehicles.

This required fundamental reshaping of market perceptions and expectations. Traditional wisdom held that electric vehicles were inherently compromised – environmentally-friendly but inferior in performance, range, and desirability. Tesla's genius lay in recognizing that this assumption itself created an opportunity. Rather than accepting the conventional trade-off between sustainability and performance, they engineered a new market position that transformed these apparent contradictions into advantages.

Tesla's vacuum creation involved three interconnected dimensions. First, they undertook systematic market education, teaching consumers to see electric vehicles not as ecological compromises but as superior driving machines. This wasn't merely marketing – it required demonstrating previously unimagined capabilities, from instant torque delivery to over-the-air software updates that improved vehicles over time.

Second, they created entirely new infrastructure paradigms. The Supercharger network wasn't just about charging cars; it represented a fundamental reimagining of how vehicles could be refueled. Their direct-to-consumer sales model didn't merely bypass dealerships; it created new standards for how cars could be bought and serviced. Each element was carefully engineered to support and reinforce their created vacuum.

Third, they undertook sophisticated value engineering that redefined how consumers evaluate vehicle ownership. They introduced new metrics for performance that highlighted electric vehicles' advantages while creating novel financing and ownership models that aligned with these new value propositions. The result wasn't just a new product; it was an entirely new category of vehicles that consumers hadn't known they wanted until Tesla showed them it was possible.

This case demonstrates how created vacuums require fundamentally different capabilities than natural ones. While natural vacuum fillers need exceptional execution capabilities, vacuum creators must excel at market education, infrastructure development, and value redefinition. They must not only deliver solutions but also teach the market to value them appropriately.

This distinction between finding existing gaps and creating entirely new ones first clicked for me during a retail innovation workshop in Singapore. A young entrepreneur asked, 'Are we solving problems people know they have, or creating solutions they don't yet realize they need?' That seemingly simple question perfectly captured what separates natural vacuums from created ones. It made me think differently about every market opportunity I encountered afterward."

Chapter 2

The Five Types of Market Vacuums

Understanding the Different Spaces of Opportunity

Understanding market vacuums is much like understanding different types of weather patterns. Just as meteorologists can predict storms by recognizing specific atmospheric conditions, business leaders can spot opportunities by understanding distinct vacuum types. This meteorological parallel runs deeper than mere analogy. Like weather systems, market vacuums form through the interaction of multiple forces, create recognizable patterns before fully manifesting, and can be either naturally occurring or artificially induced.

Consider how a meteorologist analyzes the formation of a hurricane. They don't just look at one factor like wind speed or air pressure – they study the interaction of multiple conditions: water temperature, atmospheric pressure gradients, wind patterns, and seasonal timing. Similarly, identifying market vacuums requires understanding how different business conditions interact to create opportunities. Just as different types of storms require different prediction models and response strategies, different types

9

of market vacuums demand distinct approaches to identification and exploitation.

The weather analogy extends even further when we consider the predictability and intervention possibilities. Just as humans have learned to seed clouds or build hurricane-resistant structures, businesses can learn to not just spot but actively engineer market vacuums. Understanding these different types of vacuums – their formation patterns, characteristic signals, and optimal response strategies – provides business leaders with a powerful framework for opportunity identification and market creation.

In my extensive research across industries and timelines, I've identified five distinct types of market vacuums, each with their own characteristics, formation patterns, and strategic implications:

1. *Feature Vacuums*: These emerge when existing products or services lack crucial capabilities that could create significant value.

2. *Experience Vacuums*: These occur when functional solutions exist but fail to meet deeper emotional or experiential needs.

3. *Price Vacuums*: These develop in the gaps between existing price points, where significant market segments remain underserved.

4. *Access Vacuums*: These form when value exists but remains unreachable for significant market segments.

5. *Trust Vacuums*: These emerge when existing solutions suffer from fundamental confidence gaps.

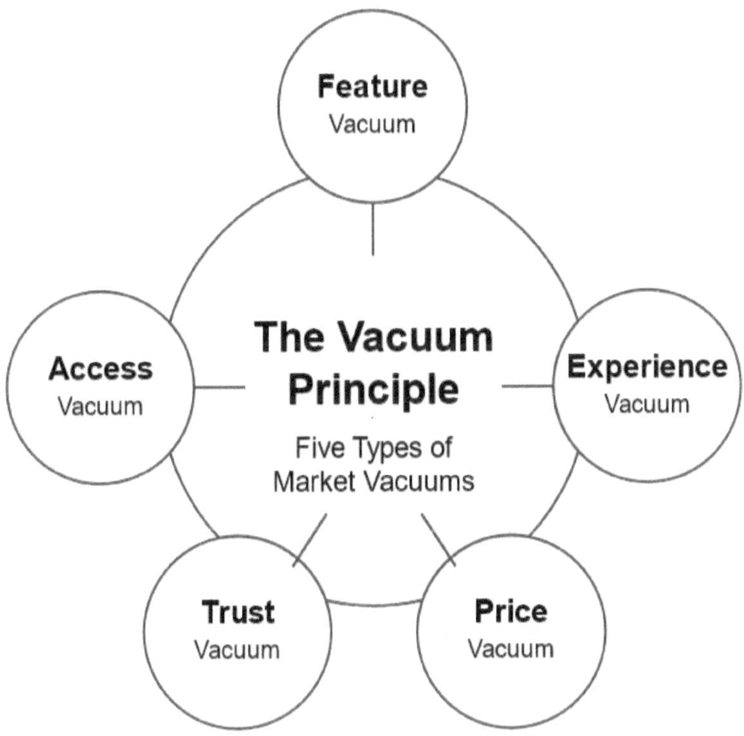

Each of these vacuum types requires different identification methods, filling strategies, and defensive approaches. In the following sections, we'll explore each type in detail, examining how they form, how they can be spotted, and most importantly, how they can be successfully filled and defended with examples. Understanding these distinct types of market vacuums provides business leaders with a sophisticated toolkit for identifying and capturing opportunities that others miss.

I first began mapping these distinct vacuum types while studying market transformations in emerging economies. What started as a pattern recognition exercise during consulting projects and business advisory work gradually evolved into a comprehensive framework as I noticed how successful companies were consistently exploiting these different types of gaps, often without explicitly recognizing the underlying patterns themselves. The more I studied these successes, the clearer these five fundamental types became.

Let's begin by examining the first and perhaps most visible type: Feature Vacuums.

1. Feature Vacuums: The Innovation Gap

Feature vacuums are often the most visible yet frequently misunderstood market gap. They appear straightforward – something is missing, so add it. But it's rarely that simple.

Consider how Apple approached Touch ID. The feature vacuum wasn't just about fingerprint security; it was about reimagining device interaction entirely. When they introduced Touch ID in 2013, they weren't merely solving a security problem. They were addressing several interconnected needs:

The Anatomy of Feature Vacuums:

Primary Function: Immediate practical need

- The core problem being solved must be significant enough to drive adoption. With Touch ID, the immediate need was simplifying device security. Users were frustrated with constantly entering passcodes, often leading them to disable security features entirely.

- This primary function must be executed flawlessly. Apple's implementation was remarkably reliable, working in milliseconds and from multiple angles.

- The solution should feel inevitable – once users experience it, going back should feel unthinkable.

Secondary Benefits: Unexpected advantages

- Great feature vacuums often reveal unexpected benefits after launch. Touch ID quickly became valuable for in-app purchases, making them frictionless yet secure.

- These secondary benefits often create more value than the primary function. The payment authentication capability became central to Apple Pay's success.

- Users typically discover these benefits organically, leading to deeper platform engagement.

Future Potential: Platform for innovation

- Strong feature solutions create foundations for future innovations. Touch ID established biometric authentication as a norm, paving the way for Face ID.

- They enable new business models. The security feature enabled new financial services opportunities.

- They create opportunities for ecosystem expansion. Developers could use the technology for their own authentication needs.

Integration Value: Ecosystem enhancement

- Feature solutions should strengthen the entire product ecosystem. Touch ID made every Apple service more secure and convenient.

- They should create synergies across products and services. The feature worked seamlessly across devices and applications.

- The integration should enhance the overall platform value proposition, making switching costs higher.

User Experience: Behavior modification

- Successful feature solutions often change user behavior patterns. People became comfortable with biometric authentication in daily life.

- They create new habits that become standard expectations. Users now expect instant, secure authentication everywhere.

- These behavioral changes often ripple beyond the immediate use case, influencing broader market expectations.

This power to reshape user behavior is vividly demonstrated by two transformative innovations: Amazon Prime and Apple AirPods.

Let's dive deep into them.

Examples of Future Vacuums:

1. Amazon Prime: The Reinvention of Customer Loyalty

In 2005, Amazon stood at a crucial crossroads. Their e-commerce business was growing, yet they faced a significant challenge: shopping cart abandonment due to shipping costs. This was a common problem in the online retail space, and conventional wisdom suggested simple solutions like lowering shipping fees or offering occasional free shipping promotions. However, Jeff Bezos and his team saw beyond the surface-level issue. They identified a deeper vacuum in the market, one that would revolutionize not just online shopping, but consumer behavior as a whole.

Instead of merely addressing the shipping cost problem, Amazon created Prime – a service that, at its inception, appeared to be a straightforward subscription for free two-day shipping. But the genius of Prime lay in its recognition that the real vacuum wasn't just about shipping costs; it was about removing all friction from the online shopping experience.

The evolution of Amazon Prime over the years tells a fascinating story of how a company can continually expand to fill an ever-growing market gap. In 2005, when Prime launched, it offered free two-day shipping for an annual fee of $79. This alone was a game-changer, encouraging customers to shop more frequently on Amazon, knowing they wouldn't face additional shipping charges.

But Amazon didn't stop there. They understood that to truly dominate the retail space, they needed to become an indispensable part of their customers' lives. In 2011, they added a streaming video service to Prime, directly competing with Netflix and transforming Prime from a shipping service into an entertainment platform. This move was strategic – it increased the perceived value of Prime and gave customers another reason to remain loyal to Amazon.

The additions continued at a rapid pace. In 2014, Amazon added music streaming and unlimited photo storage to Prime. These features not only added value but also deepened Amazon's integration into their customers' daily lives. Prime was no longer just about shopping; it was becoming a comprehensive digital lifestyle service.

2016 saw the introduction of Prime Wardrobe, allowing customers to try on clothes before buying, and the integration of grocery services. This move into fashion and fresh food demonstrated Amazon's ambition to capture every aspect of retail. By 2017, same-day delivery became available in major markets, further reducing the gap between online and physical retail.

In 2019, Amazon raised the bar again by making one-day shipping the standard for Prime members. This move not only delighted customers but also put immense pressure on competitors, widening the vacuum Amazon had created and continued to fill.

What started as a $79 annual subscription for free shipping had transformed into a comprehensive lifestyle service that fundamentally changed consumer behavior. Prime members began checking Amazon first for any purchase, knowing they'd get fast, free delivery along with a host of other benefits. The service created what we might call a "feature cascade" – each new addition made the next one more valuable and increased the overall stickiness of the Prime ecosystem.

The genius of Amazon Prime lies in its ability to continually identify and fill new vacuums in the market. By bundling an ever-expanding array of services under one subscription, Amazon has created a loyalty program that goes far beyond points or rewards. They've built a ecosystem that customers find increasingly difficult to leave, ensuring Amazon's position at the center of their shopping and entertainment lives.

2. Apple AirPods: The Silent Revolution in Audio

When Apple announced in 2016 that they were removing the headphone jack from the iPhone, the public reaction was largely negative. Critics called it a mistake, even labeling the decision as arrogant. But Apple, true to its innovative spirit, had identified a feature vacuum that others hadn't seen: the messy and often frustrating relationship between humans and audio devices.

Traditional wireless headphones had solved only part of the problem – they eliminated the wire. But Apple saw several deeper issues that plagued the user experience of personal audio devices. The frustration of Bluetooth pairing was a common complaint among users of wireless headphones. The process was often unintuitive, requiring multiple steps and sometimes failing for no apparent reason. This created a barrier to entry for many users who might otherwise have been interested in wireless audio.

Another issue was the awkwardness of carrying cases. Traditional earphones, whether wired or wireless, often ended up tangled in pockets or bags. This not only created a nuisance for users but also led to damaged earphones and shortened product lifespans. Apple recognized that a seamless storage solution was just as important as the earphones themselves.

The interruption caused by taking earphones in and out was another pain point Apple identified. Whether answering a call, speaking to someone briefly, or just pausing music, the process of removing and reinserting earphones was cumbersome. This interruption in the user experience was a vacuum ripe for innovation.

The complexity of managing multiple devices was yet another issue. Many users had different headphones for different devices – perhaps one set for their phone, another for their computer, and maybe even a third for their television or gaming system.

This not only added cost and clutter but also created friction in moving between devices.

Lastly, Apple recognized the poor integration of existing headphones with voice assistance technologies. As virtual assistants like Siri became more prevalent, the need for seamless interaction between audio devices and these AI helpers became more apparent.

Apple's solution to these problems came in the form of AirPods, and it was comprehensive. The H1 chip (initially the W1 chip in the first generation) allowed for instant device recognition. This solved the Bluetooth pairing issue, making the connection process as simple as opening the AirPods case near an iPhone. The seamless pairing extended to all devices on the user's iCloud account, effectively solving the multi-device management problem as well.

The AirPods also featured automatic ear detection. This clever feature allowed the earphones to automatically pause audio when removed from the ear and resume when reinserted, addressing the interruption issue. It made the experience of using AirPods feel more natural and integrated into the user's behavior.

Gesture controls for different functions added another layer of convenience. Users could double-tap to activate Siri, play or pause music, or skip tracks. This feature evolved in later generations to include squeeze gestures on the stems, providing even more control without the need for physical buttons.

The case that doubled as a charger was a stroke of genius. It solved the storage problem, keeping the AirPods safe and untangled, while also ensuring they were always charged and ready for use. The small, pocket-friendly design of the case made it easy for users to carry their AirPods everywhere, increasing usage and user satisfaction.

The result wasn't just a pair of wireless earbuds; it was a new paradigm for how we interact with audio and our devices. AirPods created a more seamless, intuitive audio experience that felt almost like a natural extension of the user's hearing. Sales grew multifold, creating a new product category that others rushed to join.

The success of AirPods demonstrates the power of identifying and filling a *feature vacuum*. By addressing not just one, but a whole series of interconnected user pain points, Apple created a product feature that transformed the personal audio landscape. The AirPods story is a testament to the idea that true innovation often comes not from creating something entirely new, but from reimagining and improving the way we interact with technology we use every day.

The Feature Vacuum Framework: Five Essential Questions

I've found that successful feature vacuum identification comes down to five key questions. Let's examine each through the lens of our Amazon Prime and Apple AirPods examples:

1. What are people struggling with, even if they're not complaining? This question helps identify underlying pain points that consumers may have accepted as unavoidable.

For Amazon Prime:

- Customers silently accepted shipping costs as an unavoidable tax on online shopping

- Cart abandonment due to shipping fees was considered a normal part of e-commerce

- Unpredictable delivery times were seen as inherent to online retail

- Multiple small shipping charges created friction in purchase decisions

- Waiting for orders to meet free shipping thresholds was an accepted hassle

2. What secondary benefits could emerge from solving the main problem? This question encourages thinking beyond the immediate solution to identify additional value that could be created.

When creating AirPods, Apple saw potential for numerous secondary benefits beyond just wireless audio:

- Seamless device switching solved the problem of managing multiple audio connections

- The charging case addressed battery life concerns while providing convenient storage

- Automatic ear detection allowed for more intuitive control

- Integration with Siri improved access to voice assistance

3. What behaviors would change if this problem disappeared completely? This question helps envision the broader impact of solving a particular problem.

Amazon Prime's elimination of shipping costs and delivery friction changed consumer behavior in several ways:

- Increased frequency of online purchases

- Shifted consumer expectations for delivery speed across all e-commerce

- Made Amazon the first-choice destination for online shopping

- Normalized subscription-based loyalty programs

4. Why aren't current solutions perfect? This question pushes us to critically examine existing solutions and identify areas for improvement.

   In analyzing wireless earphones, Apple identified several imperfections:

   - Unreliable Bluetooth pairing processes

   - Poor integration between devices

   - Lack of intuitive controls

   - Battery life and charging limitations

   - Awkward storage solutions

5. How would this feature evolve if there were no constraints? This final question encourages bold, long-term thinking about potential evolution.

   Amazon Prime demonstrates this evolutionary thinking perfectly. From its initial shipping benefit, it has grown to encompass:

   - Entertainment streaming services

   - Cloud storage

- Shopping benefits across multiple retail categories

- Rapid delivery options

- Integrated payment systems

By continually asking how their services and products could evolve without constraints, both Amazon and Apple have transformed their initial solutions into comprehensive platforms that touch multiple aspects of consumers' lives. The Feature Vacuum Framework, through these five questions, provides a powerful tool for identifying and developing innovative features.

By applying this framework, companies can move beyond solving immediate problems to reshape entire markets and consumer behaviors, creating expanding vacuums that drive continuous growth and innovation.

2. Experience Vacuums: The Emotional Gap

Experience vacuums are often the most powerful yet subtle type of market opportunity. While feature vacuums address what people need, experience vacuums address how people feel. They exist in the space between functional adequacy and emotional satisfaction.

Every time I visit a Starbucks store, I'm struck by how masterfully they convert a simple commodity - coffee - into a comprehensive experience. The carefully curated music, the familiar aroma, the comfortable seating, the personalized greeting - none of these elements are about the coffee itself, yet they're fundamental to why people choose Starbucks. When they introduced the concept of a "third place," they weren't merely selling coffee; they were addressing several interconnected emotional needs.

The Anatomy of Experience Vacuums:

Primary Connection: Emotional Core Need

- The emotional need must resonate deeply enough to drive behavior change. With Starbucks, the core need was a space between home and work.

- This emotional connection must feel authentic. Starbucks created environments that felt simultaneously productive and relaxing.

- The experience should feel personal yet universal – something everyone can relate to but make their own.

Secondary Elements: Sensory Integration

- Great experience vacuums engage multiple senses. The coffee aroma, comfortable seating, curated music, and warm lighting work together.

- These sensory elements often create more value than the primary product. The atmosphere became more valuable than the coffee itself.

- Users should discover new aspects of the experience over time, deepening engagement.

Community Creation: Social Framework

- Strong experience solutions build community naturally. Starbucks baristas remembering regular customers' names and orders.

- They enable both connection and privacy. Store layouts provide communal tables and private corners.

- They create shared rituals and language. The "Grande Latte" ordering ritual became part of daily life.

What makes experience vacuums particularly fascinating is their compound effect.

When Starbucks filled this vacuum, they:

Created a New Social Space:

- Beyond traditional coffee shops

- More than a quick service restaurant

- Different from bars or cafes

- Not quite work, not quite leisure

- A unique hybrid that met multiple needs

Established New Consumer Behaviors:

- Premium coffee became everyday luxury

- Working in cafes became normal

- Coffee breaks evolved into social occasions

- Personal customization became expected

- Take-out coffee became a fashion statement

This power to shape emotional connections and create new social frameworks is powerfully demonstrated by two transformative cases: Disney's reimagining of family entertainment, and Peloton's revolution in home fitness.

Let's dive deep into them.

Examples of Experience Vacuums:

1. The Disney Theme Parks: Reimagining Family Entertainment

    In 1955, Walt Disney embarked on a revolutionary journey to transform the landscape of family entertainment. At a time when American families had numerous entertainment options, including carnivals, circuses, and amusement parks scattered across the country, Disney perceived a significant vacuum in the market. While these existing venues offered thrills and games, Disney envisioned something profoundly different: a place where magic came to life, and where parents and children could share authentic emotional moments together.

    The genesis of this vision came from a deeply personal experience. As Walt Disney watched his own daughters enjoy a carousel ride, he found himself sitting on a nearby bench, eating peanuts, and feeling oddly disconnected from their joy. This moment of reflection sparked the realization that there was a profound experience vacuum in family entertainment. The existing model of amusement parks often segregated experiences, with children enjoying rides while parents watched from the sidelines. Although families weren't explicitly complaining about this arrangement, Disney recognized it as a hidden pain point in family outings.

    Disney's solution to this unspoken problem went far beyond merely creating new rides or attractions. He set out to craft an immersive experience that would engage every family member, regardless of age. This approach required reimagining every aspect of the traditional amusement park model.

One of the key innovations was in the park's staff, known as Cast Members. Unlike traditional amusement park employees who were primarily trained in ride operations and basic customer service, Disney's Cast Members were trained in the art of storytelling. They were taught to view themselves as integral parts of the park's narrative, with each interaction serving to enhance the overall magical experience for guests. This approach transformed simple transactions or directions into opportunities to deepen the immersive experience.

The commitment to maintaining the illusion of a perfect, magical world led to innovative operational practices. Maintenance work, for instance, was scheduled to happen invisibly before dawn. This ensured that guests never saw the behind-the-scenes work that kept the park running, preserving the seamless magical experience throughout their visit. This attention to detail extended to every aspect of the park's design and operation.

Visual design was another area where Disney's approach differed significantly from traditional amusement parks. Every visual angle within the park was carefully considered and crafted to contribute to the overall thematic experience. This meticulous attention to detail ensured that guests were fully immersed in the park's various themed lands, with no jarring elements to break the illusion.

Even seemingly minor elements like background music were given careful consideration. The soundtrack of the park was designed to change subtly as guests moved between different areas, enhancing the sense of place and story in each themed land. This auditory layer added depth to the immersive experience, often working on a subconscious level to enhance guests' emotional engagement with their surroundings.

Disney's innovative approach extended to the most mundane aspects of park operations. Even trash cans were reimagined to fit seamlessly into the themed environments. Rather than being eyesores that detracted from the magical atmosphere, they were designed to complement their surroundings, often incorporating thematic elements that made them attractions in their own right.

The impact of Disney's innovations transcended the realm of entertainment. By creating a space where families could make memories together, Disney established a new category of destination. The park wasn't just a place to visit; it became a pivotal part of family traditions and a backdrop for cherished memories. This emotional connection to the Disney experience has proven to be a powerful force, driving repeat visits and fostering a deep loyalty to the Disney brand.

Today, Disney theme parks worldwide welcome approximately 150 million visitors annually. These guests don't simply come to ride attractions; they come to immerse themselves in stories, to step into fantastical worlds, and to experience magic firsthand. The success of Disney's approach is evident not just in these impressive attendance figures, but in the way Disney has become synonymous with family entertainment and magical experiences.

The Disney theme park case study demonstrates the power of identifying and addressing hidden emotional needs in the market. By reimagining family entertainment from the ground up, Disney didn't just fill an existing gap – they created an entirely new category of experience.

2. Peloton: Transforming Solo Exercise

By 2012, the landscape of home fitness had become a veritable graveyard of good intentions. Across America, treadmills were repurposed as makeshift clothes hangers, and exercise bikes gathered dust in corners, silent testimonies to abandoned New Year's resolutions. It was in this environment of fitness disillusionment that John Foley, the founder of Peloton, identified a crucial insight: the problem wasn't with the equipment itself, but with the solitary, uninspiring experience of exercising alone at home.

Foley and his team embarked on a journey of deep customer research, seeking to understand the underlying reasons for the failure of home fitness equipment. What they uncovered was a complex web of interconnected issues that went far beyond the mere functionality of exercise machines.

One of the primary findings was that people deeply missed the energy and motivation that came from group exercise classes. The camaraderie, the shared struggle, and the collective achievement that characterized gym classes were entirely absent from the home exercise experience. This social element, it turned out, was a crucial factor in maintaining long-term exercise habits.

Moreover, home exercisers reported feeling disconnected and unmotivated. Without the structure and guidance of a class environment, many found it challenging to push themselves or maintain consistency in their workouts. The absence of external motivation often led to half-hearted sessions or, worse, complete abandonment of exercise routines.

Time constraints emerged as another significant barrier to maintaining a fitness regimen. Many people expressed a desire to attend gym classes but found it increasingly difficult to align their busy schedules with fixed class times. The commute to and from the gym added another layer of complexity, making regular attendance a logistical challenge for many.

Quality instruction, Peloton's research revealed, was often geographically limited. While major urban centers might offer a plethora of expert-led fitness classes, those in smaller towns or rural areas had limited access to top-tier instruction. This disparity in access to quality guidance was a significant factor in the fitness divide.

Perhaps most importantly, the research highlighted the crucial role of social accountability in maintaining a fitness routine. The commitment made to a gym buddy or a regular class acted as a powerful motivator, one that was sorely missing in the solitary world of home exercise.

Armed with these insights, Peloton set out to create a solution that would address each of these pain points, ultimately giving birth to an entirely new category in the fitness industry. Their approach was revolutionary in its comprehensive reimagining of the home exercise experience.

At the heart of Peloton's innovation was the concept of live classes led by charismatic instructors. These weren't pre-recorded, one-size-fits-all videos, but dynamic, real-time sessions that brought the energy of a gym class directly into people's homes. The instructors, carefully selected for their expertise and motivational skills, quickly became celebrities in their own right, building loyal followings among Peloton users.

To address the lack of competition and benchmarking inherent in solo workouts, Peloton incorporated real-time metrics into their platform. Users could see their performance data on screen, comparing their output to both their personal bests and to other participants in the class. This feature created a natural sense of competition, pushing users to improve their performance and stay engaged throughout the workout.

Recognizing the importance of community in maintaining exercise motivation, Peloton built robust social features into their platform. Users could connect with friends, join groups based on shared interests or fitness goals, and participate in challenges together. This virtual community recreated the sense of belonging and mutual support typically found in physical gym environments.

Performance tracking was another key element of Peloton's solution. By providing detailed data on each workout, including metrics like distance covered, calories burned, and power output, Peloton gave users tangible evidence of their progress over time. This data-driven approach not only provided a sense of achievement but also drove accountability, encouraging users to maintain consistent workout habits.

Perhaps most importantly, Peloton preserved the convenience factor that initially drew people to home exercise equipment. The flexible schedule of live and on-demand classes meant that users could work out whenever it suited them, eliminating the time constraint issues associated with traditional gym classes.

The result of this comprehensive approach was nothing short of transformative. Peloton evolved from a quirky startup with an unusual idea to a fitness phenomenon valued at $32 billion at its peak. By identifying and filling an experience vacuum in connected fitness, Peloton not only revitalized the home exercise equipment market but created an entirely new category of fitness product.

Peloton's success story demonstrates the power of deeply understanding customer needs and pain points. By addressing not just the functional aspects of exercise but the emotional and social components as well, Peloton created a product that resonated deeply with consumers. Their approach transformed the solitary act of home exercise into a communal, motivating, and ultimately sustainable fitness experience.

The Experience Vacuum Framework: Five Essential Questions

The successful experience vacuum identification comes down to five key questions. Let's examine each with clear examples from Disney and Peloton:

1. What emotional needs remain unmet in functional solutions? This question helps identify underlying emotional needs that consumers may not explicitly express but deeply desire.

   Disney Parks demonstrates this perfectly:

   - Traditional amusement parks focused only on individual rides and attractions

   - Families weren't explicitly asking for immersive experiences

- Parents often felt disconnected from their children's enjoyment

- Entertainment was segmented rather than shared

- The magic of childhood wasn't being captured systematically

2. How could this experience create a genuine community? This question encourages thinking beyond the immediate service to identify opportunities for fostering meaningful connections.

Peloton exemplifies this approach. The primary need was to create an effective home exercise solution. However, Peloton saw potential for numerous community-building benefits:

- Live classes created a sense of shared experience and motivation

- Leaderboards and performance tracking enabled friendly competition

- User profiles and social features allowed riders to connect

- Instructor-led sessions fostered a sense of belonging

By considering these community aspects, Peloton created a product that went far beyond just being an exercise bike, instead offering a comprehensive fitness ecosystem.

3. What deeper human connection is missing? This question helps to envision the broader impact of creating more meaningful, authentic interactions.

Disney Parks illustrates this through their systematic approach:

- Transformed staff from ride operators into storytellers and magic-makers

- Created opportunities for shared family moments at every touchpoint

- Designed spaces that encouraged multi-generational interaction

- Built experiences that parents could enjoy alongside children

- Engineered moments of wonder that brought families closer together

4. How could this transaction become a transformation? This question focuses on how to elevate single interactions into life-changing experiences.

   Peloton demonstrates this by transforming the basic act of exercise:

   - Turned solitary workouts into shared community achievements

   - Converted daily exercise from obligation into inspiring ritual

   - Transformed fitness metrics into personal growth stories

   - Made home workouts feel as engaging as boutique fitness classes

   - Created a sense of belonging in what was traditionally an isolated activity

5. What lasting impact could this experience have? This question examines how to build enduring institutional and cultural influence.

Disney Parks exemplifies this through systemic impact:

- Created a new category of family entertainment that influences generation after generation

- Built an operational model that became the global standard for themed entertainment

- Developed technologies and practices that revolutionized the entire entertainment industry

- Established new standards for employee training and guest service across industries

- Engineered experiences that became cultural touchstones and family traditions

By continually asking how their services could evolve and create lasting value, both Disney and Peloton have transformed their initial solutions into comprehensive platforms that reshape entire industries. The Experience Vacuum Framework, through these five questions, provides a powerful tool for identifying and developing transformative experiences.

3. Price Vacuums: The Value Gap

In every market, a spectrum of price points and value propositions forms a pyramid-like structure. At the base are mass-market products, followed by mid-range offerings, premium products, and luxury items at the apex. This price-value pyramid is dynamic, with astute companies identifying and filling gaps, creating new market segments and redefining consumer expectations.

The automotive industry illustrates how companies have consistently filled price vacuums across this spectrum. Initially, cars were luxury items for the wealthy elite. Henry Ford recognized this gap and revolutionized the industry with the Model T, making car ownership possible for the average American.

As the market matured, companies identified more nuanced price vacuums. Toyota created Lexus, challenging the notion that luxury cars must be European. BMW's Mini found space between economy and premium, creating a new category of premium small cars. Tesla entered at the luxury end before moving downstream with the Model 3. Hyundai's Genesis brand identified a vacuum in "accessible luxury."

In emerging markets like India, Maruti Suzuki dominated the mass-market segment before launching Nexa to fill a growing premium segment vacuum.

This principle extends beyond automotive. In any market, we can apply this pyramid model to identify potential gaps. It's akin to Newton's third law: for every low-priced product, there's potential for a premium or luxury counterpart. If such an offering doesn't exist, it often signals an unmet need.

By viewing markets through the lens of this price-value pyramid, businesses can uncover hidden opportunities. The key is not just to make products cheaper or more expensive, but to identify unserved price-value combinations that resonate with specific consumer segments. As we'll explore further, this approach to finding and filling price vacuums can lead to innovative products, new market categories, and significant competitive advantages.

Of all the vacuum types I've explored, price vacuums have always fascinated me the most. Perhaps it's because, as a consumer, I've watched countless purchasing decisions - my own and others' - pivoted on that delicate balance between price and value. I've seen how people will stretch their budgets for certain brands while refusing to pay premium prices for others. This consistent pattern has shown me that price isn't just about affordability - it's about perceived worth and positioning. When companies get this balance right, they can create entirely new market segments that seemed impossible before.

The Anatomy of Price Vacuums:

Value Architecture: Segment Innovation

- Each market segment has unique price-value equations. What represents value to a luxury consumer differs fundamentally from mass-market expectations. For instance, luxury consumers might value exclusivity and craftsmanship, while mass-market consumers prioritize functionality and reliability.

- Price positions must align with clear value delivery. Lexus didn't just offer lower prices than Mercedes; it delivered a different kind of luxury experience centered on reliability and customer service – qualities underserved in traditional luxury segments.

- Market positioning should bridge recognizable gaps rather than force new segments. Tesla identified the gap between luxury performance and environmental consciousness, creating a natural bridge between seemingly opposing values.

Price-Value Alignment: Perception Management

- Price vacuums exist where value perception and price points misalign. The success of Warby Parker demonstrated how designer eyewear could be both affordable and fashionable, challenging the notion that high prices equal high style.

- Premium products can find vacuums by democratizing access. Apple's iPhone SE brought flagship phone capabilities to mid-range price points without diluting the brand's premium positioning. This created a new entry point for aspirational consumers while maintaining the brand's overall value proposition.

- Mass market products can find vacuums through premium variants. Starbucks Reserve elevated the everyday coffee experience to new price points by offering unique beans, brewing methods, and environments – creating a luxury coffee experience within a mass-market brand.

- Luxury offerings can find vacuums through accessibility. Net-a-Porter transformed luxury fashion retail by removing the intimidation factor of high-end boutiques while maintaining the premium shopping experience through careful curation and white-glove service.

Category Definition: Market Space Creation

- Successful price vacuum fills often create entirely new categories. Away Luggage created the premium direct-to-consumer luggage category by offering luxury quality at mid-market prices through a new business model.

- They redefine what's possible at specific price points. Dollar Shave Club proved that premium razors could be affordable through subscription models, changing expectations about what quality costs.

- They challenge existing segment boundaries. Peloton merged luxury fitness equipment with affordable personal training, creating a new hybrid category that didn't exist before.

- They create new consumer behaviors. Rent the Runway changed how people think about fashion ownership by making luxury clothing accessible through rental, creating new consumption patterns at multiple price points.

The principles of price vacuums come alive through real-world transformations. Let's examine how Lexus and Royal Enfield masterfully filled price gaps to create entirely new market categories.

Examples of Price Vacuums

1. Lexus: Redefining Luxury Value

In 1989, the luxury car market was characterized by clear boundaries. European brands dominated the sector, relying on their heritage and commanding high prices, while mass-market brands catered to everyone else. Toyota, however, identified a crucial vacuum in this landscape: a segment of successful professionals who desired luxury but defined it differently. These consumers sought reliability, cutting-edge technology, and exceptional customer service rather than just prestige.

Toyota's extensive market research unveiled a series of key insights that would shape their approach. Luxury car buyers were growing increasingly frustrated with the poor reliability and frequent repairs that often accompanied their high-end vehicles. The dealer service experience was consistently disappointing, with many customers feeling they were treated arrogantly or dismissively. Moreover, there was a growing realization among consumers that the high price tag of luxury vehicles didn't necessarily reflect quality in the actual ownership experience.

The research also revealed a shift in the luxury market demographic. New money was entering the sector, and these buyers were looking for different status symbols beyond the traditional European heritage. They were more open to innovative approaches and fresh interpretations of luxury. Additionally, Toyota recognized that technology could be a significant luxury differentiator, not just an expensive add-on.

Another critical insight was the disparity in customer experience across dealerships. Traditional luxury dealers often treated servicing as a profit center rather than an integral part of the luxury experience. This resulted in widely varying levels of service quality, which was at odds with the premium positioning of the brands.

Armed with these insights, Toyota set out to create Lexus, a brand that would redefine luxury in the automotive world. The Lexus solution was comprehensive and revolutionary, addressing each of the identified pain points in the luxury car market.

At the core of the Lexus proposition was an unmatched commitment to reliability. The brand set unprecedented quality standards, targeting zero defects in their vehicles. This approach was a direct response to the frustration luxury buyers felt with frequent repairs and maintenance issues.

Lexus also reimagined the dealer experience. They introduced a revolutionary approach that included services like pickup and delivery for vehicle maintenance, eliminating the inconvenience traditionally associated with car servicing. This was complemented by an industry-first loaner car program as a standard offering, ensuring that Lexus owners were never without a luxury vehicle.

Technology played a central role in the Lexus value proposition. Advanced features that were often expensive options in other luxury brands became standard in Lexus vehicles. This approach positioned Lexus as a technology leader in the luxury segment, appealing to buyers who valued innovation.

The brand's pricing strategy was innovative. Lexus introduced value pricing for premium features across their range, challenging the notion that luxury had to come with an exorbitant price tag. This approach made luxury more accessible to a broader range of consumers while still maintaining a premium positioning.

Design-wise, Lexus successfully blended Japanese precision with luxury aesthetics. This unique approach to luxury design set Lexus apart from its European counterparts and resonated with buyers looking for a fresh interpretation of automotive luxury.

Perhaps one of the most significant innovations was Lexus's approach to customer relationships. The brand introduced personal relationship managers for each customer, creating a level of personalized service unprecedented in the automotive industry. This was coupled with a comprehensive warranty program that exceeded industry norms, further emphasizing Lexus's commitment to customer satisfaction.

The impact of Lexus's entry into the luxury car market was profound and far-reaching. Within two years of its launch, the Lexus LS was outselling both the Mercedes S-Class and BMW 7-Series, a clear indication that the brand had successfully tapped into an unmet need in the market.

Lexus effectively created a new category of "reliable luxury," forcing traditional luxury brands to improve their quality and reliability to remain competitive. The brand's innovative approach to dealer service transformed expectations industry-wide, elevating the importance of the ownership experience in the luxury segment.

Moreover, Lexus established a new benchmark for customer satisfaction in the automotive industry. Their focus on creating a consistent, high-quality experience across all touchpoints influenced how luxury cars are evaluated and sold globally. The brand's success prompted a shift in the entire industry's approach to quality control and customer service.

In essence, Lexus's entry into the market didn't just fill a price vacuum; it redefined what luxury meant in the automotive context. By understanding and addressing the unmet needs of luxury car buyers, Lexus created a new paradigm that continues to influence industry today. Their story serves as a powerful example of how identifying and filling a price vacuum with unique value can lead to new category creation.

2. Royal Enfield: Reviving Heritage to Fill the Mid-Premium Motorcycle Vacuum

In the early 2000s, the Indian motorcycle market was sharply divided. On one end were the mass-market commuter bikes, dominated by brands like Hero MotoCorp and Bajaj, offering affordable transportation to the masses. On the other end were high-end, expensive imported motorcycles like Harley-Davidson, catering to the luxury segment but out of reach for most Indian consumers. Between these extremes, Royal Enfield, a company with a rich heritage but struggling sales, identified a significant price vacuum: the mid-premium segment.

During a consulting engagement with the Tata Group in Pune in 2023, I spent time with a local Royal Enfield riders' club and witnessed firsthand how brilliantly the company had identified and filled this vacuum. What struck me most wasn't just their market positioning, but how they had created an entire cultural movement in a space that didn't exist two decades ago. The transformation from a struggling heritage brand to a cultural icon perfectly illustrates the power of identifying and filling a price vacuum.

This strategic positioning allowed Royal Enfield to tap into a previously underserved consumer base. While Harley-Davidson served the top layer luxury market of the pyramid, and Indian brands like Bajaj and Hero MotoCorp served the mass market and mid segment, Royal Enfield found its unique price positioning in the growing premium segment in the Indian market.

Royal Enfield recognized that there was a growing class of Indian consumers who desired more than just basic transportation. These riders wanted motorcycles that offered a blend of style, heritage, and performance, but at a price point that was accessible to the upper-middle class. This vacuum represented an opportunity to create a new category in the Indian motorcycle market.

The company's research revealed several key insights:

Indian riders were developing a strong interest in leisure motorcycling, moving beyond mere commuting. There was a growing nostalgia for classic designs and a desire for bikes with character. Many consumers aspired to own premium motorcycles but found imported brands like Harley-Davidson prohibitively expensive. The market lacked options that combined power, style, and affordability in a way that bridged the gap between mass-market offerings and luxury imports.

Armed with these insights, Royal Enfield set out to fill this price vacuum with a strategic approach:

They revived and modernized their classic designs, maintaining the iconic look while improving performance and reliability. The company positioned their bikes as lifestyle products rather than mere transportation, appealing to the emotional aspirations of riders. Royal Enfield priced their motorcycles significantly below imported premium brands but above mass-market commuters, creating a distinct mid-premium category that set them apart from both Harley-Davidson and the likes of Bajaj and Hero MotoCorp.

The brand focused on building a strong community around their products, organizing rides and events that fostered a sense of belonging among Royal Enfield owners. They expanded their dealership network and improved their after-sales service to enhance the ownership experience.

The result of this strategy was transformative, both for Royal Enfield and the Indian motorcycle market. Sales grew exponentially, from around 25,000 units in 2005 to over 800,000 units by 2018. Royal Enfield successfully created and dominated the mid-premium motorcycle segment in India, effectively filling the gap between mass-market players and luxury imports.

By identifying and filling the premium price vacuum, Royal Enfield not only revived its own fortunes but also reshaped the Indian motorcycle market.

The Price Vacuum Framework: Value Creation Across Segments

1. Where does price prevent value delivery? This question encourages companies to identify barriers where pricing structures inhibit the delivery of value to potential customers.

   Royal Enfield identified that high prices of imported premium motorcycles were preventing many Indian consumers from accessing quality riding experiences. By introducing bikes at an accessible mid-premium price point, they made premium motorcycling available to a broader market.

   - Designing an operations model that enables sustainably lower prices

   - Identifying which elements create core value for the target market

   - Building infrastructure that supports high-volume efficiency

   - Developing revenue streams that don't compromise core value

   - Creating replicable service standards for scale

2. What premium value remains unserved? This question prompts businesses to look for opportunities to deliver premium value in ways that haven't been explored by existing market players.

   Lexus exemplifies this approach in the luxury car market. They identified that reliability, advanced technology, and superior customer service were premium values that remained largely unserved by traditional luxury car brands. By focusing on these aspects, Lexus created a new definition of luxury in the automotive industry.

   - Aligning product features with unmet premium needs

   - Developing differentiated service elements

   - Creating a unique market space beyond price point

   - Building a comprehensive premium ecosystem

   - Designing a scalable premium experience

3. How can value perception be shifted? This question encourages companies to think about ways to change how customers perceive value in their industry.

   Royal Enfield's success in the Indian motorcycle market illustrates this principle. They shifted the value perception of motorcycles from mere transportation to lifestyle products. By emphasizing heritage, design, and community, Royal Enfield changed how Indian consumers viewed mid-premium motorcycles.

   - Developing strong value-quality messaging

   - Creating a memorable product experience

- Building trust through consistent delivery

- Establishing clear brand benefits

- Maintaining high-quality standards at scale

4. Where can new price-value equations work? This question prompts businesses to explore innovative pricing models that can create new value propositions.

   Lexus challenged traditional luxury car pricing by offering advanced features as standard equipment while maintaining prices below European competitors. Their innovative approach made luxury more accessible while preserving premium positioning.

   - Designing authentic brand experiences

   - Developing an innovative distribution model

   - Creating sustainable competitive advantages

   - Building a long-term value proposition

   - Maintaining brand integrity at scale

5. How can price innovation create new categories? This final question encourages thinking about how pricing strategies can lead to entirely new market categories.

   Royal Enfield created an entirely new mid-premium motorcycle category in India, positioning themselves between mass-market commuters and luxury imports. This strategic pricing approach not only revived their brand but reshaped the entire Indian motorcycle market.

- Building a robust supporting ecosystem

- Designing for profitable scale

- Developing sustainable unit economics

- Controlling critical value chain elements

- Creating powerful network effects

The Price Vacuum Framework, through these five questions, provides a powerful tool for identifying and developing innovative pricing strategies. By applying this framework to the examples of Lexus and Royal Enfield, we can see how these companies were able to create products and services that went beyond solving immediate pricing issues to reshape entire markets and consumer behaviors.

4. Access Vacuums: The Accessibility Revolution

Traditional markets often define opportunities through product features or price points. However, some of the most profound market transformations come from companies that identify and fill fundamental gaps in accessibility and distribution. Access vacuums exist where value is present but remain unreachable for significant market segments.

These vacuums represent untapped potential in markets where the primary barrier is not the product itself, but the means by which consumers can obtain or experience it. Companies that successfully identify and fill these vacuums often create disruptive innovations that reshape entire industries.

I've experienced this reality repeatedly in my consulting work with modern D2C brands. One particular instance stands out - while advising a promising premium personal care startup,

I watched their initial success hit a hard ceiling. Despite strong product reviews and growing online demand, they couldn't match the market presence of traditional players. I noticed their products were consistently absent from shelves where P&G, Unilever, and other established brands maintained a constant presence.

This distribution gap wasn't just about logistics - it represented a fundamental access vacuum that even the most innovative D2C brands struggle to fill. Their availability remained mostly restricted to e-commerce platforms, while conventional consumer companies maintained their powerful moat through deep retail penetration. It was a vivid reminder that in consumer businesses, physical availability (access) is just as important as product superiority.

These distribution gaps, or access vacuums as I call them, exist across many markets beyond D2C, presenting rich opportunities for entrepreneurial innovation and growth.

The Anatomy of Access Vacuums

Access vacuums are complex structures that, when successfully filled, can revolutionize entire industries and reshape consumer behaviors. To understand how companies can identify and leverage these opportunities, we need to dissect the anatomy of access vacuums. This analysis reveals four key components: Access Architecture, Value Liberation, Scale Dynamics, and Trust Framework.

1. Access Architecture: Barrier Removal

    The foundation of any access vacuum is the existence of barriers that prevent consumers from easily obtaining or experiencing value. These barriers can take various forms, but they generally fall into three categories: physical, time-based, and systemic.

Physical barriers often involve geographic limitations or the need for physical presence. Amazon Prime's success stemmed from its ability to remove the physical distance between consumers and products. By offering fast, free shipping, Amazon made a vast array of products accessible to consumers regardless of their location, effectively shrinking the perceived distance between desire and fulfillment.

Time barriers constrain access based on schedules or time zones. Traditional banking hours, for instance, limited access to financial services. The rise of digital banking removed these constraints, allowing consumers to manage their finances at any time, from anywhere. Similarly, educational platforms like Coursera have made learning accessible across time zones and personal schedules, liberating education from the constraints of traditional classroom hours.

Systemic barriers are often deeply ingrained in existing infrastructure or processes. M-Pesa in Kenya provides a powerful example of overcoming systemic barriers. By bypassing traditional banking infrastructure, M-Pesa provided financial services to the unbanked population, demonstrating how innovative access solutions can leapfrog existing systems to serve underserved markets.

2. Value Liberation: Unlocking Existing Value

Access vacuums often exist not because value is absent, but because it's trapped behind barriers. The process of filling these vacuums involves liberating this existing value and making it more readily accessible.

Spotify exemplifies this concept in the music industry. The value – the music itself – already existed. Spotify's innovation was in making this vast library of music easily accessible through streaming technology. This not only liberated existing value but also multiplied it by allowing users to access a much wider range of music than they could practically own.

LinkedIn demonstrates how improving access can multiply value. Professional networks have always been valuable, but by making these connections visible and accessible digitally, LinkedIn dramatically increased the value of existing professional relationships and created new opportunities for networking.

3. Scale Dynamics: Access Amplification

The power of access solutions often lies in their ability to scale, which can amplify their impact and value.

Network effects play a crucial role in many access solutions. Platforms like Uber become more valuable as they grow – each new driver and rider increases the utility of the service for all users. This scalability can create powerful momentum, rapidly expanding the accessibility of the service.

Successful access solutions often leverage existing infrastructure to scale quickly. Instagram, for instance, built its platform on the foundation of smartphone cameras and mobile networks, allowing it to rapidly scale its photo-sharing service without having to build physical infrastructure.

The development of supporting ecosystems is often crucial for the scalability of access solutions. Tesla's investment in its Supercharger network illustrates this principle. By building out charging infrastructure, Tesla made electric vehicles truly accessible for long-distance travel, addressing a key barrier to adoption.

4. Trust Framework: Confidence Building

Trust is a critical component of access vacuums, particularly when new models of access are being introduced.

Digital payment platforms had to overcome significant trust barriers to gain widespread adoption. This involved not only ensuring the security of transactions but also building user confidence in a new way of handling money.

Verification systems are often crucial in enabling new forms of access. Digital signatures and identity verification technologies have been key to enabling remote access to a wide range of services, from banking to government services.

New access models often require innovative approaches to risk management. Airbnb, for example, had to develop comprehensive insurance and verification systems to build trust between strangers and enable its peer-to-peer rental model.

The transformative effect of filling access vacuums extends far beyond the immediate service or product. It can redefine industries, create new behaviors, redistribute value, evolve entire ecosystems, and have significant social impacts. From the way Kindle transformed publishing and reading habits to how educational platforms have democratized learning, the effects of successfully filling access vacuums ripple out across society, reshaping how we live, work, and interact with the world around us.

When it comes to putting these principles into practice, two transformative examples stand out. Let's explore how Dell and

UPI broke through established barriers to revolutionize access to computers and financial services.

Examples of Access Vacuums

1. Dell: Revolutionizing Computer Access through Direct Distribution

In the early 1990s, the personal computer market was dominated by a traditional retail model. Consumers typically purchased pre-configured computers from retail stores, often dealing with limited choices, outdated technology, and inflated prices due to the multi-layered distribution system. Michael Dell identified a significant access vacuum in this market – consumers lacked direct access to customizable, up-to-date computer systems at competitive prices.

Dell's innovative approach to filling this access vacuum transformed not just the company, but the entire PC industry. Let's examine the key elements of Dell's strategy:

1. Direct-to-Consumer Model: Dell revolutionized computer sales by eliminating the middleman. By selling directly to consumers, Dell removed a significant barrier between customers and the product. This direct model allowed customers to order customized computers tailored to their specific needs, a level of personalization that was previously unavailable in the mass market.

2. Build-to-Order Manufacturing: Dell implemented a build-to-order system that allowed computers to be assembled only after a customer placed an order. This approach solved several access issues simultaneously:

- It eliminated the need for large inventories, reducing costs and allowing Dell to pass these savings on to customers.

- It ensured that customers always had access to the latest technology, as Dell could quickly incorporate new components into their offerings.

- It provided customers access to a wide range of configuration options without the limitations of pre-built systems.

3. Online Configuration and Ordering: As the internet gained popularity, Dell leveraged this new technology to further enhance accessibility. The company launched one of the first comprehensive e-commerce websites, allowing customers to configure and order their computers online. This move significantly expanded Dell's reach, making their products accessible to anyone with an internet connection.

4. Just-in-Time Inventory: Dell's just-in-time inventory system was crucial in maintaining their competitive edge. By keeping minimal inventory and working closely with suppliers, Dell could offer the latest technology at competitive prices. This system allowed Dell to provide customers with access to cutting-edge components faster than traditional retail channels.

5. Direct Relationship with Customers: By selling directly to consumers, Dell gained valuable insights into customer needs and preferences. This direct relationship allowed Dell to rapidly adapt to changing market demands, further enhancing their ability to provide relevant, accessible products.

6. Corporate and Institutional Focus: Dell didn't limit its direct model to individual consumers. The company also focused

on providing easy access to customized computer systems for businesses and institutions, filling a significant vacuum in the corporate IT market.

The Impact of Dell's Access Innovation:

Dell's approach to filling the computer access vacuum had far-reaching effects:

1. Industry Transformation: Dell's direct model forced other PC manufacturers to reconsider their distribution strategies, leading to industry-wide changes.

2. Price Reduction: By cutting out middlemen and optimizing operations, Dell made powerful, customized computers more affordable and accessible to a broader market.

3. Customization Norm: Dell's success made customization an expected feature in the PC market, changing consumer expectations.

4. Supply Chain Innovation: Dell's just-in-time inventory system became a model for efficient supply chain management across industries.

5. E-commerce Pioneer: Dell's online ordering system was at the forefront of e-commerce, paving the way for online retail in other sectors.

Dell's case study demonstrates how identifying and filling an access vacuum can lead to disruptive innovation and industry-wide transformation. By reimagining how consumers could access and purchase computers, Dell not only built a successful company but also changed the dynamics of the entire PC industry.

2. India's UPI (Unified Payment Interface): Revolutionizing Financial Access in the Digital Age

In the realm of digital payments and financial inclusion, India's Unified Payments Interface (UPI) stands out as a remarkable success story in filling a critical access vacuum. While even advanced economies have struggled to create seamless, universally accessible digital payment systems, India has managed to leapfrog many developed nations in this arena, providing a compelling case study of innovation in addressing accessibility challenges.

I'm a big fan of India's UPI system, having watched firsthand as a user how it elegantly simplifies transactions in the country's complex banking ecosystem. What started as a solution to India's digital payments challenge has evolved into perhaps the world's most sophisticated yet easy-to-use financial interface.

Before UPI's introduction in 2016, India faced a significant digital divide in financial services. A large portion of the population, particularly in rural areas, remained unbanked or underbanked. Even among those with bank accounts, digital transactions were often cumbersome, requiring smartphones, stable internet connections, and complex apps. This created a substantial vacuum in the rapidly digitalizing economy.

The architects of UPI recognized these barriers and set out to create a system that would work for all Indians, regardless of their technological sophistication or economic status. The result was a payment interface that was simple, interoperable, and accessible even on basic feature phones.

What makes UPI's success particularly noteworthy is how it contrasts with the experiences of many developed countries. In the United States, for instance, digital payment systems remain fragmented, with various apps and platforms competing for market share but often lacking interoperability. European countries have made strides with systems like SEPA, but widespread adoption of real-time, mobile-first payment solutions has been slower.

UPI, on the other hand, created a unified system that works across all banks and financial institutions. A user can send money to anyone else instantly, knowing only their UPI ID, without needing to know their bank details. This simplicity and universality were key to its rapid adoption.

The impact of UPI in filling the digital payment access vacuum has been profound. The growth of UPI transactions has been nothing short of extraordinary. In the financial year 2022-2023, UPI processed a staggering ₹139 lakh crore (approximately $17 trillion) in transaction value. This represents a phenomenal 168% increase from ₹1 lakh crore in FY 2017-18, just five years earlier. This explosive growth not only demonstrates the rapid adoption of UPI but also highlights its crucial role in bringing millions of previously excluded individuals into the formal financial system.

UPI's success can be attributed to several key factors that addressed different aspects of the access vacuum:

1. Simplicity: UPI made digital transactions as easy as sending a text message, removing the complexity barrier that deterred many from adopting digital payments.

2. Interoperability: By allowing transactions between any bank accounts, UPI eliminated the silos that previously existed in digital payment systems.

3. Inclusivity: UPI works on basic feature phones as well as smartphones, making it accessible to a broader segment of the population.

4. Cost-effectiveness: By making peer-to-peer and merchant payments free or very low cost, UPI removed a significant financial barrier to digital transactions.

5. Government support: Strong backing from the Indian government and the Reserve Bank of India provided the necessary regulatory framework and push for adoption.

6. Open architecture: UPI's design allowed for the development of numerous apps and services, fostering innovation and further enhancing access to financial services.

The transformative impact of UPI extends beyond just facilitating payments. It has become a platform for financial inclusion, enabling easier access to banking services, credit, and investment opportunities for millions of Indians. Small businesses, which often struggled with the costs and complexities of traditional payment systems, have found in UPI a tool for growth and formalization.

Moreover, UPI's success has inspired other countries to consider similar models. Countries like Singapore, the UAE, and several African nations have shown interest in adopting UPI-like systems, recognizing its potential to address their own financial access vacuums.

The Internet: The Ultimate Access Vacuum Filler

The advent of the internet has fundamentally transformed how we access information, goods, and services, effectively filling numerous access vacuums across various sectors. E-commerce platforms have revolutionized retail, making a vast array of products accessible to consumers worldwide with just a few clicks. These platforms have not only simplified shopping but also democratized market access for small businesses and individual sellers.

Content platforms such as YouTube, Spotify, and Netflix have revolutionized entertainment and education, allowing creators to reach global audiences directly. This has led to an explosion of diverse content and niche markets that were previously underserved by traditional media.

Social media platforms have transformed how we connect, share ideas, and build communities. They've become powerful tools for spreading new ideas, mobilizing social movements, and fostering innovation through global collaboration.

Crowdfunding platforms such as Kickstarter have democratized access to capital, allowing individuals and small organizations to fund projects, causes, and startups that might have struggled to find support through traditional channels.

The rise of direct-to-consumer (D2C) brands, facilitated by e-commerce and social media, has disrupted traditional distribution models. Companies can now reach customers directly, bypassing costly intermediaries and established retail networks. This has significantly lowered entry barriers for new brands and products, fostering innovation and competition.

Moreover, the internet has enabled the rapid spread of new ideas and innovations. Open-source platforms, online forums, and collaborative tools have created a global ecosystem of knowledge sharing and co-creation, accelerating the pace of innovation across industries.

In essence, the internet has become the ultimate tool for filling access vacuums. It has removed geographical constraints, lowered economic barriers, and democratized opportunities across numerous sectors. By enabling direct connections between creators, producers, and consumers, it has challenged traditional gatekeepers and empowered individuals and small entities to compete on a global stage.

However, this digital revolution also presents new challenges, such as digital divide issues, privacy concerns, and the need for digital literacy. As we continue to leverage the internet to fill access vacuums, addressing these challenges will be crucial to ensure that the benefits of this digital accessibility are equitably distributed.

The Access Vacuum Framework: Breaking Barriers to Reach

The Access Vacuum Framework provides a structured approach to identifying and addressing gaps in accessibility across various sectors.

This framework consists of five key questions that help uncover opportunities to improve access and create value. Let's examine each question using examples from Dell and UPI that have filled access vacuums:

1. What fundamental barriers prevent value delivery? This question encourages identifying the core obstacles that prevent people from accessing products, services, or information.

   Dell identified that traditional retail distribution models prevented customers from accessing customizable, up-to-date computers at competitive prices. By eliminating middlemen and creating a direct-to-consumer model, Dell made powerful computing accessible to a broader market.

- Building direct relationships with customers

- Designing efficient distribution models

- Creating scalable access points

- Removing intermediary barriers

- Enabling customization at scale

2. How can technology bridge the access gap? This question prompts exploration of how emerging technologies can be leveraged to improve accessibility.

    UPI demonstrates this principle perfectly. By leveraging mobile technology and creating a unified payment interface, UPI made digital financial services accessible to millions of Indians, regardless of their bank or device type.

- Developing interoperable systems

- Creating universal standards

- Building robust infrastructure

- Ensuring inclusive design

- Leveraging existing technology

3. What unconventional channels can reach underserved markets? This question encourages thinking beyond traditional distribution models to reach new audiences.

    Dell pioneered online configuration and ordering when the internet was still emerging, creating a new channel that dramatically expanded access to customized computers. Their direct model became a blueprint for e-commerce.

- Identifying alternative distribution paths

- Creating new delivery models

- Developing innovative platforms

- Building direct connections

- Establishing new standards

4. How can existing resources be repurposed for broader access? This question focuses on leveraging existing assets or infrastructure in new ways to improve accessibility.

   UPI repurposed India's existing banking infrastructure by creating an interoperable layer that connected all banks and payment providers. This approach made digital payments accessible without building entirely new banking systems.

- Leveraging existing networks

- Integrating current systems

- Transforming available resources

- Creating connection layers

- Building on proven foundations

5. What systemic changes can create sustainable access? This final question encourages thinking about long-term, structural changes that create lasting improvements in accessibility.

   Dell's build-to-order manufacturing system and just-in-time inventory management created a sustainable model for delivering customized computers at scale. Similarly, UPI's open architecture and government backing established a lasting foundation for digital payments in India.

- Developing sustainable models

- Creating scalable systems

- Building lasting infrastructure

- Establishing industry standards

- Engineering for future growth

The Access Vacuum Framework, through these five questions, provides a powerful tool for identifying and developing innovative solutions to accessibility challenges. The transformative examples of Dell and UPI demonstrate how removing barriers to access can reshape entire industries and create new paradigms for value delivery.

5. Trust Vacuums: Bridging the Confidence Gap

In our increasingly interconnected world, the flow of value is no longer confined to the digital realm. It transcends industry boundaries, weaving through diverse business models and sectors. Yet, at the heart of this interconnected landscape, a fundamental challenge persists: how can people, organizations, and institutions place their trust in what they cannot directly see, touch, or verify?

These trust vacuums emerge when the potential for value creation remains untapped, as stakeholders hesitate to engage, transact, or collaborate due to a lack of confidence. Whether it's consumers reluctant to make online purchases, businesses wary of outsourcing critical operations, or communities skeptical of new technologies, the inability to establish trust can keep billions of dollars in potential value locked away.

The Anatomy of Trust Vacuums:

Confidence Architecture: Verification and Transparency Innovation

Filling trust vacuums requires innovative approaches to building confidence and mitigating perceived risks. This goes beyond merely implementing secure systems - it involves creating trust signals that align with clear risk mitigation strategies. Successful trust vacuum fillers understand that trust must be designed as meticulously as any product feature or operational process.

For instance, when Marriott entered the hospitality industry, they didn't just focus on providing high-quality accommodation. They engineered a comprehensive loyalty program that fostered a sense of community and exclusivity, giving customers confidence in the long-term reliability of their brand experience. Similarly, Tata Group in India systematically built trust across their diverse business operations, creating a reputation for social responsibility and national development that transcended their individual product and service offerings.

Risk Management Framework: Uncertainty Reduction and Transparency

Successful trust vacuum fillers recognize that perceived risks must be systematically reduced to unlock value. This may involve increasing transparency, providing familiar guarantees, or simplifying complex systems. Consider how Unilever's supplier rating system in their Shakti initiative helped build confidence in the company's commitment to responsible sourcing and production, addressing the trust vacuum in rural India's distribution networks.

Community Standards: Collective Trust Building and Social Proof

Some of the most powerful trust vacuum fills emerge from the creation of self-regulating communities and new social norms that foster trust through peer-based validation and shared accountability. Amazon's user review system, for example, allowed strangers to transact with confidence by tapping into the collective feedback of the platform's buyers, addressing the trust vacuum in online marketplaces.

The Evolution Framework: Adaptive Trust Systems and Technological Integration

As markets and social expectations evolve, trust systems must continuously adapt to address new threats and opportunities. This requires balancing security with user experience, leveraging emerging technologies, and aligning with changing norms. The banking industry's transition from simple passwords to biometric authentication is a prime example of this adaptive trust framework in action, enhancing security while improving customer experience.

By mastering the principles of trust vacuum identification and filling, visionary leaders can unlock unprecedented opportunities for growth, innovation, and social impact across a wide range of industries and business contexts. The future of value creation lies not just in technology or product features, but in the ability to architect trust systems that bridge the confidence gaps between stakeholders.

Understanding these elements of trust vacuums is crucial but seeing them in action through real-world examples brings the theory to life. Let's examine how Amazon and Airbnb masterfully identified and filled trust vacuums in e-commerce and home-sharing, transforming entire industries in the process.

Examples of Trust Vacuums:

1. Amazon: Pioneering Trust in the E-commerce Frontier

In 1994, when Jeff Bezos founded Amazon, the internet was still a wild, untamed territory for most consumers. The idea of purchasing products from an unseen, virtual storefront was met with skepticism and fear. Bezos and his team faced a monumental challenge: how to convince people to trust a company they couldn't see, to buy products they couldn't touch, and to share their credit card information over this new, mysterious thing called the World Wide Web.

This wasn't just a matter of building a better website or offering lower prices. Amazon was staring into a vast trust vacuum – a chasm between the potential of online shopping and the willingness of consumers to embrace it. The company needed to build a bridge of confidence across this divide, strong enough to support the weight of billions of dollars in transactions.

Amazon's approach to filling this trust vacuum was multifaceted and evolved over time:

1. Starting Small and Focused: Amazon began by selling books, a product category with standardized quality. This choice was strategic – consumers knew what to expect from a book, reducing concerns about product authenticity or condition. By mastering this category, Amazon could build trust in its basic ability to deliver as promised.

2. Information as a Trust-Builder: The company provided comprehensive information about each book, including professional and customer reviews. This transparency helped customers make informed decisions, mimicking the experience of browsing in a physical bookstore. It was a clear signal: "We're not hiding anything. Here's all the information you need to decide."

3. Customer-Centric Policies: Amazon introduced customer-friendly policies like easy returns and refunds. This reduced the perceived risk of online purchases, effectively telling customers, "If you're not happy, we'll make it right." It was a bold move in an era when many businesses saw returns as a cost to be minimized.

4. The Power of Reviews: As Amazon expanded its product range, it introduced its now-famous customer review system. This wasn't just a feature; it was a revolution in building trust. By allowing customers to share their experiences, both positive and negative, Amazon created a community-driven trust mechanism. It was as if millions of customers were saying, "Don't just take Amazon's word for it. Take ours."

5. Expanding the Trust Umbrella: With the introduction of third-party sellers on its platform, Amazon faced a new challenge. How could it extend its hard-won trust to these unknown entities? The answer was the A-to-Z Guarantee, which protected customers when purchasing from these sellers. This policy effectively said, "You can trust these sellers because we're vouching for them."

6. Prime: Trust in Consistency The launch of Amazon Prime was about more than just fast, free shipping. It was about creating

a consistent, premium experience that customers could rely on. Prime members came to trust that their orders would arrive quickly and reliably, every time. This consistency bred familiarity, and familiarity bred trust.

7. **The AI and Machine Learning Era:** As e-commerce grew, so did the sophistication of fraudsters. Amazon invested heavily in AI and machine learning to detect and prevent fraudulent activities, both in transactions and in user reviews. This proactive approach to security has been crucial in maintaining trust as the platform has scaled to handle billions of transactions.

The impact of Amazon's trust-building efforts has been profound and far-reaching:

- E-commerce Explosion: Amazon's success in building trust helped pave the way for the broader e-commerce revolution.

- New Consumer Behaviors: Online shopping, once viewed with suspicion, became a normal part of daily life for millions.

- Raised Expectations: Amazon's focus on customer experience raised the bar for all businesses, online and offline.

- Data-Driven Decision Making: The company's use of data to build trust (through personalized recommendations, for example) has influenced how businesses across industries approach customer relationships.

As we look to the future, Amazon continues to face trust challenges, from data privacy concerns to scrutiny over labor practices and environmental impact. Yet its history demonstrates a crucial lesson: in the digital age, trust is not a destination but a journey. It must be continuously earned, reinforced, and adapted to new realities.

The Amazon story serves as a powerful reminder that the biggest opportunities often lie not in creating new products, but in bridging the trust gaps that prevent existing value from being fully realized. By systematically addressing the psychological barriers that held back e-commerce, Amazon didn't just build a successful company – it helped reshape how society thinks about commerce, convenience, and trust in the digital age.

2. Airbnb: Building Trust in the Sharing Economy

When Brian Chesky and Joe Gebbia first pitched their idea of strangers staying in other strangers' homes, investors weren't just skeptical - they were concerned about liability issues. The challenge Airbnb faced wasn't just creating a platform; it was engineering trust in an environment where every incident could destroy their entire business model.

The Trust Engineering Challenge:

Airbnb's first major crisis came in 2011 when a host's home was vandalized and ransacked. This incident threatened to destroy the trust vacuum they were trying to engineer. Their response wasn't just crisis management - it was systematic trust vacuum engineering.

One of the key elements of Airbnb's trust architecture was the secure payment system they developed. Recognizing the need to protect both buyers and sellers in these peer-to-peer transactions, the company implemented a robust payment processing framework. This allowed guests to complete bookings with confidence, knowing their financial information was secure, while also assuring hosts that they would reliably receive their earnings.

In addition to the secure payment system, Airbnb also engineered a comprehensive review system to encourage honest feedback from users. Guests were incentivized to provide detailed assessments of their experiences, including comments on the accuracy of listings, the cleanliness of accommodation, and the responsiveness of hosts. This crowd-sourced information not only helped future travelers make informed decisions, but it also created a feedback loop that motivated hosts to maintain high standards of service.

To further bolster trust, Airbnb established dedicated emergency response teams that could rapidly address any incidents or issues that arose. These teams were trained to handle a variety of situations, from property damage to guest complaints, with the goal of quickly resolving problems and preserving the integrity of the platform. Hosts and guests alike could take comfort in knowing that Airbnb had a dedicated support system in place to manage unexpected challenges.

Recognizing the inherent risks associated with home-sharing, Airbnb also developed a suite of insurance products specifically tailored to the needs of its users. This included coverage for hosts against property damage, as well as liability protection for guests in the event of accidents or injuries. By providing these safeguards, Airbnb was able to mitigate the perceived risks and give both parties greater peace of mind when engaging in transactions on the platform.

The Cultural Resistance Challenge:

Beyond practical concerns, Airbnb faced deep cultural resistance. The idea of staying in strangers' homes or letting strangers into your home seemed alien to many. Their solution was to engineer a cultural vacuum through systematic trust building.

They created detailed host guides and standards to ensure a consistent, quality experience for guests. These guidelines covered everything from listing accuracy and property cleanliness to host responsiveness and communication. By setting clear expectations, Airbnb was able to build trust in the reliability and professionalism of its host community.

They also developed professional photography services to help hosts showcase their accommodation in the best possible light. This not only improved the visual appeal of listings but also reinforced the notion that these were legitimate, high-quality properties rather than informal, haphazard arrangements. The carefully curated imagery helped to bridge the gap between the perceived risks of home-sharing and the reality of Airbnb's offerings.

To further cultivate trust, the company organized community meetups and events for both hosts and guests. These in-person interactions allowed users to connect with one another, share experiences, and develop a sense of belonging to the Airbnb ecosystem. By fostering these personal connections, Airbnb was able to engineer new social norms around the acceptance and trustworthiness of home-sharing.

The Result: Transforming Trust in the Sharing Economy

Airbnb's trust engineering efforts proved crucial to the company's success and long-term sustainability. By systematically addressing the trust vacuums inherent in the home-sharing model, they were able to transform consumer perceptions and behaviors.

What was once seen as a risky, fringe concept became a mainstream, trusted way for travelers to experience local communities. Airbnb's verification systems, review processes, insurance protections, and community-building initiatives gave both hosts and guests the confidence to engage in these peer-to-peer transactions, unlocking tremendous value that had previously been inaccessible.

Beyond just building a successful business, Airbnb's trust architecture had a broader impact on the sharing economy as a whole. By demonstrating that trust could be engineered and scaled, they paved the way for the widespread adoption of peer-to-peer models in transportation, services, and beyond. Airbnb's approach to trust-building served as a blueprint for other companies seeking to fill critical trust vacuums and unlock new frontiers of value creation.

The Trust Vacuum Framework: Building Bridges of Confidence

The Trust Vacuum Framework provides a structured approach to identifying and addressing gaps in trust across various sectors. This framework consists of five key questions that help uncover opportunities to build confidence and create value. Let's examine each question using examples from Amazon and Airbnb that have filled trust vacuums:

1. What makes value inaccessible due to lack of trust? This question examines how trust barriers prevent stakeholders from accessing potential value.

   Amazon's early challenges in e-commerce illustrate this perfectly. When online shopping was new, customers were hesitant to share credit card information or purchase products they couldn't physically inspect. By developing secure payment systems and comprehensive product information, Amazon made online shopping feel safe and reliable.

- Establishing secure payment systems

- Creating detailed product information

- Building fraud protection measures

- Developing customer protection policies

- Engineering trust signals

2. How can scale be leveraged to build trust at the system level? This question explores how growing networks can enhance rather than diminish trust.

Airbnb demonstrates this principle powerfully. Their review system becomes more valuable with each transaction, as more users contribute to a comprehensive web of feedback and verification.

- Creating two-way review systems

- Developing identity verification processes

- Building community standards

- Establishing performance metrics

- Leveraging network effects

3. Where can process redesign and transparency enable trust? This question focuses on how operational clarity can build confidence.

   Amazon pioneered this through transparent order tracking and clear return policies. Every step of the purchase process was made visible and understandable to customers.

   - Providing real-time tracking

   - Clarifying policies and procedures

   - Making pricing transparent

   - Showing authentic reviews

   - Communicating consistently

4. How can innovative solutions bridge trust gaps? This question encourages exploring novel approaches to building confidence.

   Airbnb created innovative trust solutions like secure payment holds, host guarantees, and professional photography services to make home-sharing feel safe and reliable.

   - Developing secure payment systems

   - Creating insurance protection

   - Building verification tools

   - Establishing safety standards

   - Engineering trust mechanisms

5. What ecosystem-level factors enable sustainable trust? This final question examines the broader system elements needed for lasting confidence.

Amazon's A-to-Z Guarantee and comprehensive marketplace rules created a sustainable foundation for e-commerce trust. Similarly, Airbnb's host protection insurance and 24/7 customer service built a reliable support system for their platform.

- Building comprehensive guarantees

- Developing support systems

- Creating clear standards

- Establishing consistent policies

- Engineering lasting protections

The Trust Vacuum Framework, through these five questions, provides a powerful tool for identifying and developing innovative solutions to trust challenges. The transformative examples of Amazon and Airbnb demonstrate how building bridges of confidence can reshape entire industries and create new paradigms for value delivery.

As I reflect on trust vacuums in markets, two contrasting experiences stand out. During my decade in real estate marketing, I witnessed firsthand how an entire industry can suffer from systemic trust deficits. Before the Real Estate Regulatory Authority (RERA) regulations, delayed property handovers were common, creating deep-seated mistrust not just in individual developers but in the entire sector. While regulatory frameworks have helped rebuild some confidence, significant trust gaps remain, particularly in after-sales service. This pattern extends beyond real estate – across many service industries, customer trust remains a critical vacuum waiting to be filled.

The other side of this coin emerged during my time as Strategic Advisor to a Tata Steel subsidiary. Here, I observed trust operating at its fullest potential. What caught my attention wasn't just the strong customer relationships, but the remarkable employee loyalty in an age of frequent job changes. Witnessing professionals who had dedicated twenty or thirty years to the organization, I understood how systematically built trust creates foundations that extend far beyond customer relationships. The Tata experience showed me that when companies fill trust vacuums comprehensively, they don't just win customer confidence – they build enduring institutions that stand the test of time.

These contrasting experiences reinforce a crucial insight: trust vacuums represent not just risks being managed, but opportunities to be seized. In markets where trust is scarce, the company that can systematically build and maintain confidence often finds itself with an insurmountable competitive advantage.

Identifying Market Gaps

Key Questions to Ask

1. Feature Vacuum

"Are there missing capabilities that could create significant value?"

2. Experience Vacuum

"Does the existing solution meet emotional and experiential needs?"

3. Price Vacuum

"Are there underserved segments between existing price points?"

4. Access Vacuum

"Is value unreachable for significant market segments?"

5. Trust Vacuum

"Do existing solutions suffer from fundamental confidence gaps?"

The Interconnected Nature of Market Vacuums

As we conclude our exploration of the different types of market vacuums, it's important to recognize the interconnected nature of these various frameworks. While we've examined feature vacuums, experience vacuums, price vacuums, access vacuums, and trust vacuums as distinct concepts, the reality is that these elements often work in tandem to shape the overall market landscape.

Successful vacuum creators understand that a holistic, integrated approach is necessary to identify and fill the most impactful opportunities. A solution that addresses a clear feature vacuum, for instance, may fall short if it fails to consider the deeper emotional needs and trust requirements of the target customers. Conversely, an experience-driven offering that lacks a compelling price-value proposition or easy accessibility will struggle to gain widespread traction.

Consider a hypothetical example in the financial services industry. A fintech startup might identify a feature vacuum in the wealth management space, using advanced algorithms to provide highly personalized investment recommendations. However, this innovation would be severely limited if it didn't address the trust vacuum around data privacy and security, or the access vacuum created by the industry's historical reliance on in-person advisory services.

By aligning these various vacuum frameworks and designing solutions that seamlessly integrate feature, experience, price, access, and trust considerations, the startup could create a truly transformative offering. Customers would not only appreciate the superior investment advice but also feel confident in the platform's data protection measures and find the service easily accessible through intuitive digital interfaces.

This interconnected approach is what separates market leaders from also-rans. The ability to see these different vacuum types as complementary rather than mutually exclusive allows innovators to architect holistic solutions that address the multifaceted needs and expectations of their target customers. It's this systemic, big-picture perspective that enables the creation of market-defining products, services, and experiences that stand the test of time.

As you continue your journey of identifying and filling market vacuums, remember to always consider the bigger picture. By aligning the five diverse vacuums and designing solutions that deliver on multiple fronts, you'll unlock the true potential of *The Vacuum Principle* and position your offerings for sustainable, long-term success.

Part 2

The Vacuum Creation Framework

How to spot, engineer and time a market gap?

The preceding chapters revealed how different types of vacuums can transform markets and create extraordinary value. We've seen how Dell identified *access vacuums* in computer distribution, how Disney filled *experience vacuums* in customer experience, how Royal Enfield discovered *price vacuums* in motorcycles, how Amazon spotted distribution vacuums in retail, and how Airbnb built *trust vacuums* in hospitality.

Yet understanding vacuum types of the market is merely the beginning. The more crucial question is: How do we systematically identify and create these opportunities? While some vacuums emerge naturally through market evolution, the most valuable ones are often deliberately engineered through careful observation and systematic innovation.

In Part 2, we will address this challenge through the Vacuum Creation Framework, which tackles three fundamental challenges:

First, **how to spot vacuums in the market** (Chapter 3) before others do. This requires more than market research; it demands a systematic approach to identifying gaps between what exists and what could be. It's about seeing not just what is missing, but understanding why it's missing and whether that absence represents genuine opportunity.

Second, **how to engineer market vacuums deliberately** (Chapter 4). Sometimes the most valuable vacuums don't exist naturally – they must be created through innovative business models, new technologies, or novel customer experiences. This requires understanding how to create spaces that customers don't yet know they need.

Third, **how to time vacuum fills** perfectly (Chapter 5). Even correctly identified vacuums can fail if filled at the wrong time. The framework must help determine not just what to fill, but when to fill it.

The following chapters provide practical tools and methodologies for addressing these challenges.

The Vacuum Creation Framework

How to spot, engineer and time a market gap?

1. Spot vacuums in the market

Develop systematic approach to identify gaps in the market between what exists and what could be.

2. Engineer market vacuums

Create new market spaces deliberately through innovative business models and value propositions.

3. Find the right time

Determine the right moment to fill identified vacuums. Success depends on when, not just what to fill.

Chapter 3

Vacuum Spotting - The Systematic Approach to Identifying Market Gaps

What is Vacuum Spotting?

Vacuum spotting is the systematic practice of identifying market gaps before others do. It combines reading market pressures, uncovering hidden customer frustrations, and understanding why existing players miss opportunities.

Contrary to popular belief, *vacuum spotting* - identifying the market gaps that you can fill, is not about sudden insights or lucky observations. It is a methodical process of market analysis that successful organizations use to identify opportunities others miss. This chapter examines three critical elements of systematic vacuum spotting that, when combined, enable the consistent identification of new market opportunities.

The Three Elements of Vacuum Spotting:

1. Reading Market Pressures: The Art of Sensing Opportunity

    Understanding how to systematically identify and analyze pressure points in markets that indicate potential vacuums. This includes examining supply-demand mismatches, price point stress, service delivery gaps, and other indicators that suggest market opportunities.

2. Identifying Hidden Customer Frustrations: Beyond Surface Complaints

    Moving past explicit customer feedback to understand deeper patterns of dissatisfaction and adaptation that reveal market gaps. This involves analyzing behavioral patterns, workarounds, and unofficial solutions that customers develop.

3. Mapping Competitive Blind Spots: Understanding Industry Limitations

    Analyzing why existing players miss or ignore certain opportunities, including examining business model constraints, operational limitations, and strategic assumptions that create market gaps.

By applying these three elements of vacuum spotting, we can move beyond assumptions and develop a structured approach to consistently identifying and evaluating market opportunities. This methodical process empowers us to see what others miss and transform these insights into successful business ventures.

1. Reading Market Pressures: The Art of Sensing Opportunity

Market pressures, like atmospheric pressure, exist whether we notice them or not. The ability to read these pressures systematically – rather than accidentally – separates consistent vacuum spotters from occasional opportunity finders. Throughout my research for this book, I've noticed an interesting pattern: while most business leaders focus on analyzing their direct competitors, the real market pressures often reveal themselves in the everyday behaviors of customers and their unspoken frustrations. Learning to read these signals has consistently proven more valuable than any market research report.

Let's examine how Southwest Airlines' founders read multiple market pressures that others either missed or misinterpreted, revealing a methodology for *systematic pressure reading* that applies across industries.

Reading Supply-Demand Mismatches:

When Herb Kelleher and Rollin King examined the Texas aviation market in 1967, they observed something crucial beyond simple supply and demand. The market didn't just lack enough flights – it exhibited systematic pressure points that indicated a deeper vacuum. Less than 15% of Americans had ever flown commercially, yet surveys showed widespread desire for air travel. This wasn't merely an issue of insufficient supply; it represented a fundamental mismatch between how air travel was being offered and how potential customers wanted to consume it.

The founders noticed that existing carriers focused exclusively on business travelers and wealthy leisure passengers, creating artificial market constraints. While competitors saw this focus as strategic, Southwest's founders recognized it as a market pressure indicator – millions of potential customers were being systematically excluded not by choice, but by industry structure.

Price Point Stress Analysis:

Southwest's analysis revealed multiple price stress indicators. A flight from Dallas to Houston could cost the equivalent of a week's salary for middle-class workers, yet buses and cars filled highways between these cities constantly. This price-mobility gap created visible pressure that manifested in several ways:

- Highways showed increasing congestion

- Bus services operated at capacity

- Business travelers complained about costs

- Regional commerce was constrained by travel expenses

- Family visits were limited by transportation costs

Each indicator suggested not just high prices, but systemic price pressure that existing solutions couldn't relieve.

Service Delivery Gap Recognition:

Beyond price, service delivery patterns revealed additional pressure points. Existing airlines operated hub-and-spoke systems that prioritized network efficiency over customer convenience. This created observable pressure indicators:

Traditional airlines forced passengers to:

- Accept indirect routes through hubs

- Deal with complex booking systems

- Navigate frequent connection delays

- Manage complicated fare structures

- Accept limited flight schedules

These weren't just inconveniences – they were pressure points indicating market opportunity.

Geographic Coverage Analysis:

Southwest's founders might have noticed systematic geographic pressure by mapping existing flight patterns against population and commerce centers. Many medium-sized cities had minimal or inconvenient air service despite substantial potential demand. This geographic pressure manifested through:

- Business travelers driving long distances between cities

- Regional commerce relying on time-consuming ground transport

- Cities with sufficient population but limited air service

- Economic connections constrained by transportation gaps

- Market relationships limited by travel barriers

Capacity Constraint Indicators:

The market showed clear capacity pressure signals beyond simple seat availability. Business travelers often couldn't book flights on preferred schedules, while leisure travelers found weekend flights either unavailable or exorbitantly priced. These capacity constraints created visible pressure through:

- Consistently full flights on business routes

- Extreme peak pricing

- Limited schedule options

- Seasonal service gaps

- Restricted booking windows

Quality-Expectation Misalignment:

Perhaps most significantly, Southwest's founders recognized a fundamental misalignment between service quality and market needs. Existing carriers focused on premium service elements that many customers neither needed nor valued, while neglecting basics like reliable schedules and straightforward pricing. This misalignment created pressure through:

- Customer frustration with service complexity

- Resistance to bundled services

- Preference for simplicity over luxury

- Value perception gaps

- Service expectation conflicts

Distribution Channel Inefficiencies:

The existing distribution system, dominated by travel agents and complex booking systems, created additional pressure points:

- Limited direct booking options

- Multiple intermediary layers

- Complex fare structures

- Booking process friction

- Transaction cost inflation

Market Pressure Integration:

What made Southwest's analysis particularly powerful was their recognition that these various pressure points revealed multiple interconnected vacuums. Their genius lay in seeing how these different types of vacuums reinforced each other:

The price vacuum wasn't just about costs – it stemmed from distribution inefficiencies and service model limitations. The access vacuum wasn't merely about routes – it revealed fundamental business model constraints. The experience vacuum showed in the misalignment between customer needs and service delivery. The feature vacuum emerged in the gap between existing airline offerings and actual customer requirements. Most crucially, these issues collectively created a trust vacuum between airlines and potential customers who felt the industry wasn't serving their needs.

This integrated understanding enabled Southwest to:

- Fill the price vacuum through simplified, cost-efficient operations

- Address the access vacuum by creating direct point-to-point routes

- Solve the experience vacuum through customer-centric service design

- Close the feature vacuum by offering exactly what customers valued most

- Build trust through transparent pricing and reliable service

The Southwest case demonstrates that successful vacuum spotting requires seeing not just individual pressure points but understanding how different types of vacuums interconnect and reinforce each other. True market transformation comes from recognizing and filling these systematic vacuum patterns comprehensively.

Here is some reflection questions focused on reading market pressures, using Southwest's case as a reference point:

Reflection Questions:

1. Think about your industry: What are the observable "pressure signals" – like Southwest's congested highways and packed buses – that might indicate unmet market needs? Can you identify at least three tangible indicators that customers are settling for suboptimal solutions?

2. Where do you see quality-expectation misalignments in your market? Are there "premium" features or services that customers don't actually value, while basic needs remain unaddressed? What would a stripped-down, customer-centric solution look like?

3. How might different types of vacuums be reinforcing each other in your market? For example, could high prices (price vacuum) be connected to inefficient distribution (access vacuum) or poor customer experience (experience vacuum)?

4. Beyond obvious competitors, what alternative solutions are your potential customers using to meet their needs? What can these "workarounds" tell you about the true nature of market pressure in your industry?

Now, let's move to the second element of vacuum spotting.

2. Identifying Hidden Customer Frustrations: Beyond Surface Complaints

When Steve Jobs observed people struggling with their MP3 players in the early 2000s, he saw beyond their explicit complaints about battery life or storage capacity. What caught his attention wasn't what customers said – it was what they did. He noticed people carrying both their MP3 players and phones, constantly switching between devices, struggling with sync cables, and maintaining separate music libraries on different devices. These behavioral adaptations revealed a deeper vacuum that would eventually be filled by the iPhone.

The ability to read these hidden signals – what customers do rather than what they say – often reveals the most valuable market vacuums. Consider how Reid Hoffman discovered LinkedIn's opportunity not through market research, but by observing how professionals maintained complex systems of business cards, email folders, and personal notes to manage their professional networks. These unofficial solutions pointed to a profound vacuum in professional relationship management.

The Archaeology of Customer Frustration

Understanding hidden customer frustrations requires an archaeological approach – carefully excavating layers of behavior to reveal the underlying patterns of adaptation and compromise. Like archaeologists who reconstruct ancient civilizations from pottery shards and building foundations, market observers must piece together customer needs from behavioral fragments and adaptive patterns.

The Archaeology of Customer Frustration

Layer 1: Visible Adaptations
Observable behavioral modifications and workarounds

Layer 2: The Time Tax
Hidden time investments to compensate for gaps

Layer 3: Knowledge Burden
Unofficial expertise required to navigate the system

Layer 4: Social Networks
Informal support systems to overcome limitations

Layer One: The Visible Adaptations

The first layer consists of observable behavioral modifications – the visible ways customers adapt to market inadequacies. When Square's founders studied small business payments, they noticed merchants using elaborate systems to manage cash and check payments: separate bank runs for different types of deposits, complex recordkeeping systems for payment tracking, and unofficial credit arrangements with regular customers. These visible adaptations pointed to deeper problems in small business payment systems.

Consider how Airbnb's founders noticed travelers developing complex workarounds for affordable accommodation:

- Couch surfing networks among friends

- Extended stays with distant acquaintances

- Temporary sublets through classified ads

- House-sitting arrangements

- Exchange programs for temporary housing

Each adaptation represented not just a solution to immediate needs, but a signal of systematic market failure in short-term accommodation.

Layer Two: The Time Tax

Beneath visible adaptations lies a more subtle layer – the hidden time investments customers make to compensate for market inadequacies. When Instacart's founders studied grocery shopping patterns, they noticed working parents spending their Sunday evenings planning complex shopping strategies: mapping store layouts, coordinating family schedules, and developing backup plans for out-of-stock items. This "time tax" represented a significant hidden cost that customers had simply accepted as normal.

The time tax often manifests in elaborate planning rituals. Before Zomato (the food delivery app), Indian families and office groups developed complex systems for food delivery:

- Maintaining stacks of paper menus from local restaurants and dhabas

- Coordinating lunch orders through WhatsApp groups and email chains

- Calculating which restaurants would deliver to their area and minimum order values

- Managing a list of reliable restaurant phone numbers and preferred delivery boys

- Organizing payment collection through cash or multiple UPI transfers for group orders

These time investments weren't just inconveniences – they were signals of profound market inefficiency in India's food delivery ecosystem.

Layer Three: The Knowledge Burden

Deeper still lies the knowledge burden – the unofficial expertise customers must develop to navigate market inadequacies. When Blinkit's (a quick commerce grocery delivery start-up) founders studied India's grocery shopping landscape, they noticed how urban households built elaborate systems of knowledge to manage their daily essentials:

- Learning which local kirana stores stocked specific brands and items

- Understanding when fresh produce arrived at different shops

- Mastering optimal times to avoid queues at different stores

- Navigating multiple vendors for monthly grocery lists

- Managing relationships with shopkeepers for home delivery and credit

This accumulated knowledge represented both a barrier to convenient grocery shopping and a signal of systematic market failure in India's retail ecosystem.

Layer Four: Social Network Solutions

At the deepest level lie social network solutions – the informal networks people create to overcome professional networking limitations. Before LinkedIn, professionals developed complex social systems to manage their career connections:

- Creating alumni WhatsApp groups to share job opportunities

- Organizing informal meetups with ex-colleagues to stay updated

- Developing rotation systems for industry conference attendance to gather intel

- Maintaining shared spreadsheets of company contacts and referrals

- Building informal mentor circles for career guidance and introductions

These weren't just workarounds – they represented the creation of entire social support systems to compensate for professional networking inadequacies. Unlike the knowledge burden, which focused on individual expertise, these solutions showed how professionals had to build collective networks to advance their careers and stay informed about opportunities.

Reading the Signals: From Observation to Insight

The key to identifying hidden customer frustrations lies not just in observing adaptations, but in understanding their deeper significance. When we look closely at how people modify their behaviors, create workarounds, and develop informal systems, we see beyond immediate inconveniences. These adaptations reveal systematic market failures – gaps between what exists and what people truly need. Each small workaround, each informal solution, each community-driven fix represents not just individual coping mechanisms, but signals of larger market opportunities waiting to be filled.

Unlock the hidden customer frustrations by reflecting on these pivotal questions:

Reflection Questions:

1. What daily frustrations have you or your customers become so accustomed to that they no longer even notice them as problems? What might these adaptations reveal about unmet needs?

2. Think about a product or service you use regularly. What workarounds or informal solutions have you developed to make it work better? What might these adaptations suggest about potential improvements?

3. In your industry, what behaviors do customers routinely accept as "just the way things are"? How might these accepted limitations represent opportunities for radical innovation?

4. Can you recall a time when you or someone you know created an unofficial "hack" or solution to overcome a market limitation? What made this workaround necessary?

5. How might systematically mapping the small adaptations people make reveal larger, unaddressed vacuums in your market?

By approaching these questions with curiosity and a commitment to seeing beyond the surface, you can begin to develop the skill of spotting hidden market opportunities that others overlook.

In my years of working with entrepreneurs, I've consistently emphasized one fundamental principle: you must "get out of the building" - a phrase popularized by Steve Blank, the Silicon Valley entrepreneur who pioneered the Customer Development methodology. This mirrors the Japanese concept of *genchi genbutsu*, which encourages going to the actual place to observe real situations firsthand.

The most valuable insights I've gathered about market gaps have come not from just analyzing spreadsheets or reading market reports, but from studying people like anthropologists would - observing their natural behaviors, noticing their unconscious adaptations, and understanding their unstated frustrations. Whether it's watching how shopkeepers manage inventory in small kiranas (local street shops in India) or how office workers coordinate their lunch deliveries, these real-world observations reveal opportunities that traditional market research often misses.

For entrepreneurs looking to spot market vacuums, developing this anthropological mindset isn't just useful - it's essential.

The next big market opportunity probably isn't hidden in a market report; it's quietly waiting to be discovered in the daily workarounds and unspoken frustrations of potential customers.

Let's see the third and final element of vacuum spotting.

3. Mapping Competitive Blind Spots: Understanding Industry Limitations

As the third essential element of successful vacuum spotting, understanding industry blind spots is crucial for identifying the most impactful market opportunities. This principle is exemplified by Netflix's visionary CEO, Reed Hastings, as he envisioned the company's streaming future in 2007.

Hastings saw beyond Blockbuster's obvious limitations - it was not just what the company was doing wrong, but why they fundamentally couldn't do it right. Blockbuster's blind spots were not mere operational failures; they were deeply rooted in the structural limitations embedded within the company's business model, organizational culture, and industry assumptions. By grasping these systemic constraints, Hastings was able to devise a strategy that would prove crucial to Netflix's eventual triumph.

The Anatomy of Industry Blindness

Business Model	Organizational Capabilities
Success becomes a prison	Missing skills and systems
Mental Model	**Industry Relationships**
Fixed assumptions about business	Complex web of dependencies

The Anatomy of Industry Blindness

Industry blind spots do not emerge from incompetence, but rather from the very success that traps companies within their existing paradigms. Consider the case of Kodak, the pioneer of digital photography. Despite inventing the revolutionary digital camera, Kodak struggled to embrace the very technology it had created. Their blindness was not due to a lack of foresight; instead, their constraints were structural, woven into the fabric of their business model, organizational capabilities, and industry relationships.

1. Business Model Constraints

Often, the deepest blind spots stem from successful business models that become invisible prisons. When Amazon disrupted the book retail industry, traditional bookstores were not simply resisting change - they were shackled by their own success formula. The investments in prime real estate locations, long-term lease commitments, staff training infrastructure, and inventory display requirements were not just costs, but structural limitations that prevented these established players from envisioning, let alone pursuing, the digital opportunities that lay before them.

A similar dynamic played out in the taxi industry, where traditional companies were constrained by their medallion system. The high fixed asset costs, regulated pricing structures, geographic service limitations, vehicle maintenance requirements, and driver management systems all created blind spots about the potential for innovative, technology-driven urban transportation solutions.

2. Organizational Capabilities

Beyond the confines of business models, capability constraints - the things organizations literally cannot do due to a lack of necessary skills, systems, or culture - also contribute to industry blindness. When the disruptive home-sharing platform Airbnb emerged, traditional hotel chains were not merely ignoring the sharing economy trend; they lacked the technical capabilities, from peer-to-peer platforms to digital transaction systems, as well as the cultural mindset to participate effectively in this new market dynamic.

3. Industry Relationships

Perhaps the most binding constraints come from the complex web of partnerships, agreements, and dependencies that define how business is conducted within a particular industry. The music industry's relationship structure, for example, created blind spots around the potential of digital distribution. Exclusive dealer networks, physical retail commitments, radio station relationships, promotional agreements, and intricate rights management systems all conspired to obscure the opportunities presented by the digital revolution.

4. Mental Model Constraints

At the deepest level lie the industry-wide mental model constraints - the fundamental assumptions about the nature of the business itself. When traditional print media companies confronted the digital age, they did not merely lag in their adaptation; they were hindered by a profound misunderstanding of their core purpose. Viewing themselves as news delivery businesses, advertising platforms, and local information sources, these legacy players were unable to envision the emerging opportunities in real-time information flow, community engagement, digital content creation, and personalized delivery.

To truly internalize the power of blind spot analysis, consider the following questions that will challenge your perspective and reveal hidden market opportunities:

Reflection Questions:

1. In your industry, what are the unquestioned assumptions or practices that everyone seems to accept without critical examination? How might these be limiting innovation?

2. Can you identify a structural constraint in your current business or industry that creates a hidden opportunity for disruption? What makes this constraint so difficult for existing players to overcome?

3. Think about a successful company that fundamentally reimagined an industry. What existing constraints or "industry truths" did they challenge to create their breakthrough?

4. What organizational or cultural barriers might prevent your own organization from seeing and exploiting hidden market vacuums? How could you develop a more systematic approach to challenging these limitations?

5. If you were to approach your industry as an outsider with no preconceived notions, what fundamental practices or assumptions would you question first? What new possibilities might emerge from this fresh perspective?

Most of us ignore our competitors, but I believe studying them will show us a map of opportunity.

Every rival's move telegraphs market gaps. Every 'best practice' signals an industry blind spot. Every customer complaint is an unmet need waiting to be served.

The real art isn't avoiding competition—it's reading the competitive landscape like a treasure map and spotting market inefficiencies that are ripe for disruption.

I always joke: Our competitors aren't our enemies; they're our unwitting strategic advisors, revealing exactly where the next breakthrough lies.

Chapter 4

Vacuum Engineering - Creating Gravitational Pull in the Market

What is Vacuum Engineering?

Vacuum engineering is the deliberate creation of market spaces and business models that generate their own gravitational pull. Unlike filling existing gaps, vacuum engineers shape new opportunities that make traditional solutions obsolete.

During my research, I have observed that the art of building transformative businesses lies not just in seeing what others miss, but in reshaping entire market landscapes. While our previous chapter explored how to spot these crucial market vacuums—those telling gaps where unmet needs and inefficient workarounds signal opportunity—the true essence of market creation lies in what visionaries do next. It's about more than filling these voids; it's about engineering new spaces that fundamentally alter how markets function.

Few stories better illustrate this power of market engineering than what unfolded on a rainy evening in San Bernardino, California. A

52-year-old milkshake mixer salesman named Ray Kroc was about to witness something extraordinary. What appeared to be a simple hamburger stand would become his portal to understanding a profound business truth: markets are living ecosystems waiting to be reshaped by visionary architects.

The McDonald brothers' restaurant was already successful, serving around 125 burgers daily. But Kroc saw something even the founders of McDonald's missed—not just a local eatery, but the blueprint for an entirely new market space. This wasn't about selling more hamburgers; this was about engineering a market vacuum so powerful it would transform an entire industry.

The moment Kroc first encountered the McDonald brothers' restaurant was more than a business opportunity—it was an epiphany about the nature of market innovation. Traditional restaurants operated like artisanal workshops—unpredictable, inefficient, and deeply dependent on individual skill. They were constrained by decades of accumulated practices and unquestioned assumptions.

Where others saw limitations, Kroc envisioned an entirely new way of thinking about food, service, and human interaction. The scattered, inconsistent world of food service wasn't just ready for improvement—it was primed for complete transformation. This wasn't about creating a better restaurant; it was about engineering a new industry paradigm from the ground up.

The Essence of Vacuum Engineering

When I first began studying Ray Kroc's transformation of McDonald's, I thought I was examining a simple restaurant success story. However, deeper analysis revealed something far more profound: a masterclass in comprehensive market vacuum engineering that would reshape not just an industry, but how America eats.

The true genius of Kroc's approach wasn't in addressing a single market gap, but in his systematic orchestration of multiple vacuum types, each reinforcing the others. Like a master conductor leading a complex symphony, Kroc carefully integrated different elements to create something greater than the sum of its parts.

Vacuum Types in Action: A Systematic Transformation

Kroc's genius lay in simultaneously integrating multiple market vacuums like feature, price, experience, distribution (access), and trust that we discussed in Chapter 2. His revolutionary approach to McDonald's was far more than a simple restaurant concept. It was a meticulously engineered market transformation that simultaneously addressed multiple fundamental market vacuums, each requiring a sophisticated, nuanced approach to solving deeply ingrained industry limitations.

1. **Engineering the Fast Food Operating System**

    In the landscape of 1950s food service, restaurants operated like artisanal workshops - unpredictable, inefficient, and deeply dependent on individual skill. Kroc saw this not as a simple operational challenge, but as an opportunity to create an entirely new operating system for food service.

    The Speedee Service System represented a comprehensive transformation that addressed multiple market vacuums simultaneously:

- Custom-designed equipment and standardized processes

- Precise timing and measurement systems

- Replicable training programs

- Quality control mechanisms

2. Experience Vacuum: Reimagining Social Dining

McDonald's transcended the traditional understanding of a restaurant. It wasn't merely a place to consume food, but a carefully engineered social environment that redefined family interaction and community gathering.

The physical space was meticulously designed to create a welcoming, predictable atmosphere that invited family participation. Bright, clean environments with standardized layouts created a sense of familiarity that made customers feel at home, regardless of location. The dining experience was transformed from a transactional meal to a consistent, comforting social ritual.

Consider the psychological brilliance of this approach. In an era of increasing social fragmentation, McDonald's created a democratic space where families could gather, children could feel welcome, and the act of dining became a shared, predictable experience. The restaurant wasn't just selling food; it was selling a moment of reliability in an increasingly complex world.

Market Pull: By engineering a consistent social experience, McDonald's created a new standard that customers began to expect from all restaurants, fundamentally shifting market dynamics.

3. Price Vacuum: Economic Reimagination

Kroc's pricing strategy represented a fundamental reimagining of economic possibilities in food service. The high-volume, low-margin approach wasn't just a pricing strategy; it was an entirely new economic architecture that created natural barriers to competition.

Standardized pricing eliminated the cognitive friction of decision-making. Value meals weren't mere bundling; they were sophisticated choice simplification mechanisms. Real estate strategies weren't about location, but about creating a network of properties that supported an entirely new economic model.

The franchise system became a mechanism for rapid, controlled expansion that maintained quality and economic efficiency. Each new restaurant wasn't just a location, but a node in a complex economic network designed to generate value through scale and standardization.

System Effect: The standardized pricing model didn't just make food affordable—it created a scalable economic engine that grew stronger with each new location.

4. Access Vacuum: Democratizing Culinary Experience

McDonald's transformed dining from an inconsistent, geographically limited experience to a universal, predictable service. By creating scalable, replicable business models, they made quality food accessible across diverse locations and economic strata.

The standardization wasn't about reducing quality, but about creating a baseline of excellence that could be consistently delivered. Geographic and economic barriers dissolved as McDonald's became a universal dining experience that transcended local limitations.

Amplification Effect: Each new location strengthened the entire system, making the model more valuable for everyone in the network—customers, franchisees, and suppliers alike.

5. **Trust Vacuum: Engineering Global Confidence**

Perhaps Kroc's most profound achievement was creating a trust architecture that could transcend cultural boundaries. Every design choice - from open kitchens to consistent uniforms - was a carefully constructed trust signal.

Visual cues of reliability were universal. Transparent operational processes created a sense of authenticity. Systems were designed to feel familiar across different cultural contexts, transforming an American restaurant concept into a global institution.

Modern Impact: This systematic approach to trust-building created a blueprint for how global brands could maintain consistency while adapting to local contexts.

Creating Market Gravity

The true power of Kroc's innovation lay in how these elements reinforced each other, creating compounding effects that transformed the industry. Precision operations enabled consistent experiences, which justified standardized pricing, which funded rapid expansion, which in turn strengthened institutional trust. This wasn't just a linear progression—it was a self-amplifying system where each element catalyzed the others, creating what we might call a "gravitational pull" in the market.

While I was writing this book over the past six months, I accidentally visited McDonald's with my family for a meal. Each visit allowed me to witness firsthand how the concepts of market engineering come to life, transforming from theoretical ideas to a tangible customer experience.

How Ray Kroc Engineered McDonald's

1. Operating System
Speedee Service + Mass Production

2. Feature
Standardized Menu + Universal Product

3. Experience
Social Dining + Family-Friendly

4. Price
Value Meals + Affordable Scale

5. Trust
Open Kitchens + Quality Control

6. Access
Universal Reach + Store Network

Principles for Modern Market Engineers

1. **Design for Network Effects** Traditional businesses focus on linear growth—more locations, more customers, more revenue. True market transformation emerges from exponential dynamics, where each new addition multiplies rather than adds value. Consider how Uber's network becomes exponentially more valuable as drivers and riders join, or how Airbnb's platform grows stronger with each new host and guest. The key is identifying which elements of your business model could create similar multiplication effects. At McDonald's, each new restaurant didn't just add revenue—it strengthened the brand's reliability signal, improved supplier economics, and enhanced operational knowledge, making the entire system more valuable for everyone involved.

2. **Engineer Trust at Scale** Mass markets require trust mechanisms that work without personal oversight. The traditional restaurant model relied on individual chefs and servers to maintain quality. Kroc's genius was creating visible systems—open kitchens, standardized processes, consistent uniforms—that automatically generated trust. Modern digital platforms like Amazon and Stripe have adapted this principle, using transparent reviews, clear security badges, and visible process tracking to create trust that scales. The goal isn't to replace human elements but to create frameworks where trust becomes systematic rather than personal.

3. **Create Self-Reinforcing Value** Market transformation happens when success naturally breeds more success. Tesla's supercharger network grows more valuable with each new station, encouraging more EV adoption, which justifies more stations. Similarly, McDonald's standardized operations led

to better supplier relationships, enabling lower costs, which attracted more customers, which funded more innovation. Look for opportunities where solving one problem naturally alleviates others, creating a virtuous cycle that competitors struggle to replicate.

Understanding these principles is one thing—applying them to create market-transforming gravity is another. Let's explore how you can engineer similar forces in your own market.

Reflection Questions:

1. **System Architecture** Looking at your industry, what deeply embedded practices or assumptions are ripe for systematic reinvention? Like Kroc's reimagining of food preparation, how could you transform a current limitation into a strategic advantage?

2. **Gravitational Forces** How could different elements of your business (features, pricing, access, experience) be engineered to create self-reinforcing momentum? Consider how strengthening one aspect could naturally enhance others, creating a "gravitational pull" in your market.

3. **Scale Dynamics** Which aspects of your current business model would break under scaling, and which would become stronger? How might you redesign your systems so they don't just accommodate growth, but actively improve with scale?

The next great market transformation won't come from filling existing gaps, but from engineering new spaces that make the status quo obsolete. The potential for profound market vacuums exists in every industry, waiting for architects bold enough to realize them. The only question is: will you be the one to engineer it?

Chapter 5

Vacuum Timing - The Art of Market Entry

What is Vacuum Timing?

Vacuum timing is knowing precisely when to fill a market gap. Successful timing requires aligning three critical elements: infrastructure readiness, customer readiness, and ecosystem readiness. Like surfing, it's about catching the waves at exactly the right moment.

Great market opportunities are born from the perfect alignment of three dimensions: *spotting the right vacuum, engineering a compelling solution, and entering at the precise moment when the market is ready.* While our previous chapters explored how to identify market gaps and create powerful solutions to fill them, this chapter addresses perhaps the most subtle yet crucial element of market creation: timing.

The art of timing can mean the difference between a breakthrough innovation and a premature failure. History is filled with visionary companies that spotted the right opportunities and engineered impressive solutions, only to fall short because they moved too early or too late. Understanding when to move – and how to recognize when the market is truly ready – is often what separates successful market creators from those who end up in what Silicon Valley calls "the pioneer's graveyard."

The Pioneer's Graveyard: When Right Ideas Meet Wrong Timing

When working with founders attempting breakthrough innovations that have never existed before, I remind them of an old Silicon Valley proverb: "The pioneers get the arrows, the settlers get the land." This adage captures a painful truth about market timing. History is littered with visionary companies that spotted the right opportunities and engineered impressive solutions, only to fail because the market wasn't ready. Their stories offer crucial lessons about the importance of timing in market creation.

The Search Engine Pioneers

Before Google became synonymous with search, AltaVista stood as the pioneer of web searching. In 1995, AltaVista introduced many innovations we now take for granted - fast full-text search, natural language queries, and multimedia search capabilities. They spotted the vacuum. They engineered an impressive solution. But they were too early.

Their timing was off on three critical dimensions:

- The infrastructure wasn't ready (most people still used dial-up internet)

- User behavior hadn't evolved (people weren't yet living their lives online)

- The ecosystem was immature (digital advertising was in its infancy)

When Google arrived in 1998, these elements had aligned. The market was ready for a search revolution.

The Social Network That Came Too Soon

Friendster launched in 2002, pioneering many features that would later become fundamental to social networking. They spotted the vacuum in online social connection and engineered innovative solutions. But they were too early in three crucial ways:

- The infrastructure wasn't ready (slow internet speeds made the platform frustrating to use)

- User behavior wasn't developed (people were still uncomfortable sharing personal lives online)

- Technology ecosystem wasn't mature (mobile devices and digital cameras weren't ubiquitous)

When Facebook launched in 2004, starting with college campuses, these limitations were beginning to lift. By the time they opened to the general public in 2006, the market was primed for social networking.

The E-Commerce Pioneer's Expensive Lesson

Webvan's 1999 attempt to revolutionize grocery shopping offers perhaps the most expensive lesson in market timing. They spotted a clear vacuum (the hassle of grocery shopping) and engineered an impressive solution (automated warehouses and home delivery). They raised $800 million and built state-of-the-art infrastructure. Yet by 2001, they were bankrupt.

Their timing was off on multiple levels:

- Consumers weren't ready (people weren't comfortable buying groceries online)

- Infrastructure was immature (no smartphones for real-time delivery tracking)

- The ecosystem wasn't developed (cold-chain logistics for home delivery were in its infancy)

When Instacart launched in 2012, these elements had aligned. Smartphones were ubiquitous, people were comfortable with online shopping, and the gig economy had created a flexible delivery workforce.

The Lesson for Market Creators

These examples reveal a crucial truth: Being first isn't the same as being right. The graveyard of pioneers teaches us that timing requires the alignment of three essential elements:

1. Infrastructure Readiness - Can technology support your vision?

2. Consumer Readiness - Are people ready to embrace the change?

3. Ecosystem Readiness - Is the supporting network mature enough?

The most successful market creators aren't necessarily the first to spot a vacuum or engineer a solution. They're the ones who move when these three elements align. They understand that timing isn't just about being early or late - it's about being right.

Getting Timing Right: The Three Essential Questions

Having seen how timing failures can doom even the best innovations, we now turn to the practical challenge: How do we get timing right? The path to understanding market timing begins with recognizing that success requires more than just a great idea or excellent execution. It demands an intimate understanding of market readiness in its broadest sense.

In studying successful market creators across industries and eras, I see a clear pattern. Whether they articulated it explicitly or understood it intuitively, the victors in market creation focused relentlessly on answering three essential questions. These questions, seemingly simple on the surface, reveal deeper complexities that separate market winners from the pioneers in our corporate graveyards.

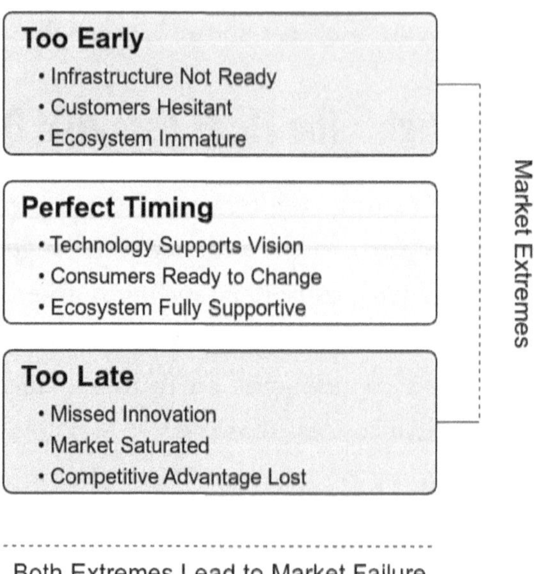

1. Infrastructure Readiness: Can the World Support Your Vision?

The question of infrastructure readiness reveals itself most clearly in Netflix's careful deliberation about streaming video in 2007. Reed Hastings and his team faced a fascinating paradox. They had successfully built the technology to stream movies over the internet. They had secured an initial library of content. Their engineers had created an impressive platform that worked flawlessly in tests. Yet they hesitated.

This hesitation reveals a profound understanding of infrastructure readiness that went far beyond their own capabilities. The Netflix team understood that their success wouldn't be determined by what they could build, but by what the world could support. They began asking deeper questions about infrastructure readiness that would shape their timing decision.

First, they looked at internet penetration and speeds across their target market. Their analysis revealed that while broadband adoption was growing, only about 20% of American households had connections fast enough for reliable video streaming in 2007. More crucially, they studied the trajectory of internet infrastructure development. They needed to understand not just current capabilities, but how quickly the infrastructure would evolve.

Beyond raw connectivity, they examined the readiness of supporting infrastructure. Could data centers handle the massive load that streaming video would create? Were content delivery networks sophisticated enough to ensure smooth playback across different regions? Would internet service providers maintain enough bandwidth as streaming traffic grew?

This deep examination of infrastructure readiness has become a hallmark of successful market timing. When Amazon launched Prime in 2005, they spent months analyzing their fulfillment network's capability to deliver on the two-day shipping promise. This wasn't just about having enough warehouses or delivery trucks. It required understanding of the entire logistics infrastructure of the country - from regional shipping hubs to last-mile delivery capabilities.

Tesla's approach to infrastructure readiness offers perhaps the most instructive example of how sophisticated market timers think about this question. When launching the Model S, they knew success required more than just building a great electric car. They needed charging stations in enough locations to make electric driving practical. They needed service centers accessible to their target customers. They needed a supply chain capable of delivering specialized components.

But Tesla's genius lay in how they approached infrastructure readiness. Instead of waiting for someone else to build charging networks, they built their own. Rather than relying on traditional auto service centers, they created a new service model. They didn't just assess infrastructure readiness - they actively shaped it.

This active approach to infrastructure points to a crucial truth about market timing: Sometimes you need to help create the infrastructure that will support your vision. The art lies in understanding how much infrastructure must exist before you move, and how much you can develop as you grow.

2. **Customer Readiness: Are People Prepared to Change?**

The second essential question delves into perhaps the most complex aspect of market timing: human behavior. Customer readiness isn't simply about willingness to pay for your offering. It's about whether people are prepared to change their behaviors in the fundamental ways your innovation often requires.

Apple's launch of the iPhone provides a masterclass in understanding customer readiness. When Steve Jobs introduced the revolutionary device in 2007, Apple wasn't just asking if people would pay a premium price for a new kind of phone. They were asking if people were ready to embrace mobile computing, touch interfaces, and app-based functionality in their daily lives.

The genius of Apple's timing lay in their recognition that previous innovations had paved the way for this behavioral shift. The iPod had already taught people to carry digital devices for entertainment. BlackBerry had established the concept of mobile email and messaging. The web was becoming mobile-friendly. People were ready for a device that would bring these elements together in a new way.

This lies in stark contrast to Google's Glass project, which failed not because of technological limitations, but because people weren't socially and culturally ready to wear computers on their faces. The behavioral leap was too great, too soon. The customer readiness simply wasn't there.

Understanding customer readiness requires a sophisticated analysis of existing behaviors and potential transitions. When Amazon introduced one-click purchasing, they weren't just offering a convenience feature. They were asking if customers were ready to trust a system with their payment information for instant purchases. This required understanding both technological trust and shopping psychology.

The most successful market timers understand that customer readiness often evolves in stages. Rather than waiting for complete readiness, they create pathways that help customers move gradually toward new behaviors. Amazon's Prime service, for instance, didn't just appear as the comprehensive benefits package we know today. It started with a simple proposition - faster shipping - and gradually expanded as customer behavior evolved.

3. Ecosystem Readiness: Is the Supporting Network in Place?

The third essential question examines the network of supporting players, complementary offerings, and environmental factors that your innovation needs to succeed. This is perhaps the most overlooked aspect of market timing, yet it often proves decisive in determining success or failure.

Uber's timing of their ride-sharing service offers a perfect case study in ecosystem readiness. Their success required the alignment of multiple ecosystem elements that weren't obvious at first glance. Smartphones had to become ubiquitous enough that both drivers and riders would have them. Mobile payment systems needed to be sophisticated enough to handle seamless transactions. GPS accuracy had to improve to the point where precise location sharing became reliable. People needed to grow comfortable with app-based services in their daily lives. The gig economy needed to emerge as a viable employment model.

What makes Uber's story particularly instructive is how they recognized that ecosystem readiness doesn't mean everything has to be perfect. When they launched, some elements of their required ecosystem were more developed than others. Their success lay in understanding which elements needed to be fully ready at launch, and which could evolve alongside their service.

Amazon Web Services (AWS) provides another masterclass in ecosystem timing. When Amazon launched AWS, they recognized that success required more than just providing cloud computing infrastructure. They needed a robust community of developers ready to build on their platform. They needed tools and frameworks that would make cloud development accessible. They needed businesses ready to trust cloud computing with their operations.

Their approach to ecosystem readiness was methodical. They started with basic services that developers could easily understand and adopt. They invested heavily in documentation and training. They built relationships with technology partners who could help companies migrate to the cloud. They didn't just launch into an ecosystem - they helped shape it.

The Power of Alignment: Finding Your Timing Window

The magic in market timing happens when these three elements align - when infrastructure can support your vision, customers are ready for change, and the ecosystem can help you grow. This alignment creates what we call the "timing window" - the optimal period for market entry and expansion.

Understanding these three questions leads us to a more sophisticated view of market timing. It's not simply about being first or waiting for perfect conditions. It's about recognizing when sufficient alignment exists to support your market entry, and understanding how to actively influence these elements to create better conditions for success.

The most successful market creators approach timing as an active, not passive, process. They don't just wait for conditions to be right - they help make them right. They build infrastructure where needed, educate customers about new possibilities, and nurture ecosystems that support their vision.

This more nuanced understanding of timing transforms how we think about market creation. It's not enough to spot a vacuum or engineer a solution. True success comes from understanding when the world is ready for your innovation, and how to actively shape that readiness to your advantage.

But how do innovators navigate the gap between perfect conditions and market opportunity? The answer lies in a strategic approach called staged entry.

Staged Entry Strategies: The Art of Imperfect Timing

The hardest truth about market timing is that perfect conditions rarely exist. When you spot a promising market vacuum and engineer a compelling solution, you'll almost always find yourself facing an uncomfortable reality: some elements are ready while others need development. The infrastructure might be available, but customers aren't ready. Or customers might be eager, but the ecosystem isn't mature. Or perhaps everything seems aligned except that one crucial element that keeps you awake at night.

This timing challenge haunts even the most promising innovations. When Reed Hastings and his team at Netflix began contemplating streaming video in 2007, they faced this exact dilemma. They had spotted a clear vacuum in entertainment delivery. They had engineered an impressive streaming platform. But broadband wasn't universal, content rights were complex, and customer behavior remained uncertain. Should they wait for perfect conditions? Risk everything on an immediate full launch? Or was there another way?

Similar questions confronted Elon Musk and the Tesla team in 2006. Electric vehicle technology was advancing, but battery costs remained high. Environmental consciousness was growing, but mass-market demand was uncertain. Charging infrastructure was minimal. Traditional market timing wisdom might have suggested waiting. Yet waiting carried its own risks – competitors advancing, technology evolving without their input, market opportunities closing.

This is the fundamental challenge of market timing: How do you move forward when conditions are promising but imperfect? When the opportunity is clear, but the path is uncertain? When waiting risks losing the opportunity, but moving too soon risks premature failure?

Imagine you're planning to swim in a cold ocean. You have two choices: jump in all at once, or wade in gradually, letting each part of your body adjust before going deeper. Staged entry in market creation is much like that gradual wading into the water. Instead of waiting for perfect conditions or plunging in completely, you enter the market step by step, each stage building upon the last.

Understanding Staged Entry

Staged entry transforms market timing from a single "go/no-go" decision into a strategic sequence of moves. Rather than launching your complete vision at once, you begin with a focused offering for a specific segment where conditions are most favorable. As you succeed in this initial space, you systematically expand both your offering and your market reach, using each stage to build the conditions for the next.

Think of it like building a bridge across a wide river. Instead of trying to span the entire distance at once, you build to the first island, establish a solid foundation, then continue to the next point, and so on. Each section makes the next one possible while also being immediately useful.

Perfect timing rarely exists in market creation. Usually, when you spot a vacuum and engineer a solution, you'll find that some elements are ready while others need development. You might have the technology, but customer behavior needs to evolve. Or customers might be ready, but the supporting ecosystem needs building. Staged entry offers a way forward in these imperfect conditions.

How Tesla Staged Its Market Entry

In the mid-2000s, the electric vehicle market was a landscape of skepticism and seemingly insurmountable challenges. Battery technology was expensive, charging infrastructure was minimal, and consumer interest was low. This was the environment in which Tesla emerged, not as a passive observer, but as an active architect of market transformation.

Tesla's approach was anything but traditional. Instead of waiting for perfect conditions, they designed a strategic staged entry that would systematically overcome market barriers and reshape automotive technology. Each stage was carefully crafted to address specific technological, economic, and perceptual challenges.

The Roadster Stage: Breaking Perceptual Barriers

When Tesla introduced the Roadster in 2008, they made a counterintuitive choice. Priced at $98,000, this high-end sports car was far from a mass-market solution. But this was precisely the point. The Roadster wasn't just a car; it was a technological manifesto that challenged every preconception about electric vehicles.

By targeting wealthy early adopters and performance enthusiasts, Tesla solved multiple strategic challenges. The high price point allowed them to absorb astronomical battery costs. More importantly, they transformed the narrative around electric vehicles from utilitarian to desirable. The Roadster proved that electric could mean high-performance, sexy, and cutting-edge—not just environmentally responsible.

Each Roadster sold was more than a revenue stream. It was a rolling demonstration of technological possibility, attracting media attention, engineering talent, and investor interest. It signaled that Tesla was a serious technological innovator capable of reimagining transportation.

The Model S: Expanding the Ecosystem

With technological credibility established, Tesla's next move was the Model S, launched in 2012. This wasn't just a new car model, but a sophisticated platform for ecosystem development. Priced in the luxury segment but more accessible than the Roadster, the Model S targeted a broader market while continuing to build critical infrastructure.

The car offered unprecedented range for an electric vehicle and sophisticated autonomous driving features. But Tesla's ambitions extended far beyond selling cars. With each Model S, they built a network of Supercharger stations that began to solve the most significant psychological barrier to electric vehicle adoption—range anxiety.

The company simultaneously collected vast amounts of real-world driving data, continuously refining battery technology, autonomous driving algorithms, and manufacturing processes. Each car sold became a research investment, bringing them closer to their ultimate goal.

The Model 3: Democratizing Electric Transportation

Only after meticulously laying the groundwork through the Roadster and Model S did Tesla launch the Model 3 in 2017—their first truly mass-market vehicle. By this point, they had transformed from a speculative startup to a formidable automotive technology company.

The Model 3 represented the culmination of a decade-long strategic journey. Battery costs had dramatically decreased, public perception had shifted, and Tesla had built a robust ecosystem of charging infrastructure, manufacturing capability, and brand recognition.

A Strategic Masterclass in Market Creation

Tesla's journey offers a profound lesson in innovative market entry. They demonstrated that market creation is not about waiting for perfect conditions, but actively shaping those conditions through strategic, staged progression. By breaking their vision into executable stages, they transformed seemingly insurmountable challenges into a roadmap for revolutionary change.

Their approach defies traditional market entry strategies. Instead of trying to solve every problem simultaneously or waiting for an imagined perfect moment, they moved forward incrementally, using each stage to build capabilities, shift perceptions, and create the very market they sought to transform.

Remember: The goal of staged entry isn't just to enter the market gradually. It's to actively shape market conditions while building your capabilities and position. Done right, it transforms timing from a single decision into an ongoing process of market development.

Staged entry might seem slower than a full-scale launch. But like the gradual wade into cold water, it often proves faster and more successful than waiting for perfect conditions or risking everything on a single plunge. It allows you to begin creating your market while actively developing the conditions for broader success.

Defense and Adaptation: Protecting Your Timing Advantage

Even the most perfectly timed market entry faces an inevitable challenge: the market never stands still. When Netflix launched streaming, competitors quickly followed. When Tesla proved electric vehicles could be desirable, traditional automakers accelerated their EV programs. When Amazon demonstrated the power of cloud computing, tech giants rushed to launch their own services.

This dynamic presents market creators with a crucial challenge: How do you protect and maintain your timing advantage when the market starts moving? How do you stay ahead when others try to copy your moves? When should you accelerate, when should you adapt, and when should you fundamentally reimagine your approach?

Think of it like sailing a ship in a competitive race. Getting a good start is crucial, but it's not enough. Wind conditions change. Competitors adjust their tactics. New challenges emerge. Success requires not just choosing the right moment to set sail, but continuously adapting to changing conditions while protecting your lead.

The Spotify Challenge: Timing in a Global Market

When Spotify launched in Sweden in 2008, they embodied the perfect market timing. Technology had reached a critical point of readiness. Music piracy had created a massive unmet demand for legal, convenient music consumption. Broadband internet was becoming ubiquitous. Young consumers were increasingly digital-native. Traditional music distribution models were collapsing.

Spotify didn't just enter the market—they reimagined music consumption entirely. Their initial proposition was revolutionary: unlimited music, instantly accessible, for a monthly fee. But perfect initial timing was just the beginning of their challenge.

As they expanded globally, they encountered a complex landscape of challenges that would test their market leadership:

- Established players rushing to launch competing services

- Rapidly evolving technology landscapes in different markets

- Shifting consumer behaviors and expectations

- Complex and changing regulatory environments

- Constant emergence of new competitive threats

Their success would depend not on their initial brilliant timing, but on their ability to defend and continuously adapt that timing advantage.

A Strategic Response

Spotify's global expansion became a masterclass in dynamic market strategy. They understood that music is deeply cultural, and their approach couldn't be a simple copy-paste of their Swedish model.

In the United States, they pioneered social listening experiences by integrating with Facebook, creating a shareable music discovery platform. In India, they developed extensive local content strategies that included regional music genres and multilingual playlists. Each market entry was a carefully researched, meticulously planned operation that respected local musical ecosystems.

Their technological strategy went far beyond simple content delivery. While competitors saw music streaming as a basic service, Spotify transformed it into an intelligence challenge. Their recommendation algorithms became increasingly sophisticated, using machine learning to predict user preferences with remarkable accuracy. This wasn't just a feature—it was a strategic moat that made their service progressively more valuable and difficult to replicate.

Recognizing the limitations of a purely music-based model, they strategically expanded into podcasts and audio content. This wasn't mere diversification—it was a preemptive reimagining of their platform's value proposition. By acquiring podcast networks and investing in original content, they transformed from a music streaming service to a comprehensive audio platform.

Defending the Timing Advantage

Spotify's defense wasn't about preventing competition—it was about continuously redefining the competitive landscape. They built network effects that made their platform increasingly valuable as more people joined. Collaborative playlists, social sharing features, and deep artist engagement tools turned listeners from passive consumers into active participants in a global musical community.

When regulatory challenges emerged in different markets, they didn't just comply—they became proactive partners in developing digital music frameworks. They invested in understanding and sometimes helping to shape the regulatory environment.

The Timing Imperative

Spotify's journey illustrates a crucial principle of market innovation: Timing is not a single moment of perfect entry, but a continuous process of alignment, adaptation, and strategic foresight.

Success doesn't come from perfectly predicting the future, but from building an organizational capability to shape and respond to emerging market dynamics. Each challenge became an opportunity to differentiate, each competitive threat a chance to innovate.

By 2020, Spotify had transformed from a Swedish startup into a global audio platform that had fundamentally reshaped how people consume music and spoken word content. Their initial timing advantage had become something far more powerful—a sustained capacity for market transformation.

From Adaptation to Offensive Strategy: The Art of Dynamic Defense

Spotify's journey reveals a fundamental truth about market leadership: survival isn't about merely defending your position, but transforming defensive challenges into opportunities for growth. Their approach of continuously reshaping the competitive landscape provides a perfect segue into understanding how the most innovative companies turn potential threats into strategic advantages.

The Principles of Dynamic Defense

1. **Monitor Multiple Horizons: The Panoramic Strategy**

    Successful market defenders possess a rare cognitive ability – the capacity to simultaneously observe and interpret market dynamics across different time scales. This isn't just about tracking competitors; it's about developing an almost prescient understanding of how market forces intersect and evolve.

Netflix's approach to this multi-horizon monitoring represents a masterclass in strategic foresight. While immediate competitors were focused on streaming content catalogs, Netflix was playing a far more sophisticated game. Their defensive strategy wasn't about protecting existing ground, but about continuously expanding their strategic perspective.

In the immediate horizon, they defended against streaming competitors by maintaining a robust and diverse content library. But their true genius lay in looking beyond the present moment. They invested heavily in original content creation, recognizing that exclusive programming would become the next battlefield in streaming wars. This wasn't a reactive move, but a proactive strategy to create a moat that competitors would find difficult to cross.

The medium-term horizon saw Netflix developing advanced artificial intelligence and machine learning capabilities. These weren't just technological investments – they were strategic weapons. By creating recommendation algorithms that could predict user preferences with unprecedented accuracy, Netflix transformed content discovery from a passive experience to an intelligent, personalized journey. Each recommendation became a subtle defensive mechanism, increasing user engagement and making platform switching increasingly unappealing.

Their long-term horizon strategy focused on international expansion and rights management. While other streaming services were primarily focused on domestic markets, Netflix was systematically building a global content ecosystem. They weren't just acquiring international rights; they were developing local content in multiple markets, creating a truly global platform that would be exponentially more difficult for regional competitors to challenge.

2. **Layer Your Defenses: The Architectural Approach**

True market leadership requires more than a single line of defense. It demands a comprehensive, multi-layered strategy where each layer reinforces and amplifies the others. Tesla's approach to defense perfectly illustrates this architectural thinking.

Their first layer of defense was continuous technological advancement, particularly in battery technology. While competitors were still deliberating about electric vehicle feasibility, Tesla was relentlessly improving energy density, charging speed, and production efficiency. Each technological improvement wasn't just an incremental upgrade – it was a strategic barrier that made catching up increasingly challenging for traditional automotive manufacturers.

The Supercharger network represented a second, equally sophisticated defensive layer. This wasn't merely infrastructure – it was a strategic ecosystem that addressed the most significant psychological barrier to electric vehicle adoption: range anxiety. By creating a comprehensive, proprietary charging network, Tesla transformed a potential weakness into a powerful competitive advantage. Each new charging station didn't just serve Tesla owners; it made the entire electric vehicle proposition more credible and appealing.

Over-the-air software updates created another innovative defensive layer. While traditional automotive companies treated cars as static products, Tesla reimagined vehicles as upgradeable platforms. A car purchased today could become demonstrably better tomorrow through software enhancements, creating a continuous value proposition that traditional manufacturers couldn't match.

Their full self-driving development represented the most forward-looking defensive layer. This wasn't just about creating autonomous driving technology – it was about positioning Tesla as a technology company that happens to make cars, rather than a traditional automotive manufacturer.

3. Convert Defense into Offense: The Transformative Mindset

The most sophisticated market defenders understand that the best defense is not about prevention, but transformation. Apple's approach to privacy concerns provides a brilliant illustration of this principle.

When privacy became a growing concern in the digital ecosystem, many tech companies saw it as a potential threat – a problem to be managed or minimized. Apple saw it differently. They recognized that privacy could be transformed from a defensive challenge into a powerful offensive strategy.

Instead of viewing privacy controls as a necessary burden, Apple reframed them as a core product feature and a fundamental brand promise. They developed privacy-focused features that went beyond industry standards, creating transparent user controls that gave individuals unprecedented insight into and control over their data.

This wasn't just a technical solution – it was a marketing masterstroke. Apple turned privacy from a technical compliance issue into a core brand differentiator. Their marketing campaigns explicitly highlighted their commitment to user privacy, positioning themselves as the most trustworthy technology provider in an increasingly complex digital landscape.

For developers, Apple created new tools and frameworks that made implementing robust privacy protections not just easy, but attractive. They transformed a potential constraint into an opportunity for innovation, encouraging developers to view privacy as a competitive advantage rather than a compliance checkbox.

The result was a paradigm shift. What could have been a defensive maneuver became a powerful offensive strategy that differentiated Apple in the marketplace, attracted privacy-conscious consumers, and forced competitors to respond to a new set of expectations about data protection.

These principles of dynamic defense reveal a profound truth: In rapidly evolving markets, the most successful companies don't just protect their position – they continuously create new opportunities from potential challenges.

Remember: Defending timing advantage isn't about building walls - it's about creating dynamic capability to stay ahead as markets evolve. Success requires not just protecting what you've built, but continuously reimagining how to maintain your lead.

The goal isn't to prevent others from following - that's usually impossible. The goal is to move forward faster than they can follow, continuously finding new ways to add value and differentiate. Done right, defense becomes not just about protecting your position, but about expanding your advantage.

If there's one lesson my years of research have consistently reinforced, it's that market leadership is fundamentally about timing. Not just the moment of entry, but the continuous dance of adaptation and growth.

I remember a conversation with a veteran entrepreneur in Singapore back in 2015 that crystallized this insight. We were sitting in a small café overlooking the city's bustling financial district, discussing the intricate art of market innovation. He compared market strategies to music – a metaphor that has stayed with me ever since.

"It's not about hitting the right note at the perfect moment," he told me, his eyes gleaming with the wisdom of decades of entrepreneurial experience. "It's about understanding the rhythm of the entire market – knowing when to wait, when to accelerate, and when to completely change the tempo."

Those words resonated deeply through my research, revealing a profound truth about market transformation.

Timing in market creation is less about prediction and more about perception. It's about developing an almost musical sense of the market's rhythm – sensing when to play softly, when to build intensity, and when to introduce a surprising note that transforms the entire composition.

The most successful innovators I've studied don't simply wait for the perfect moment. They actively shape the conditions that make their moment possible. They are simultaneously composers and performers, creating the ecosystem that will ultimately validate their vision.

Chapter 6

Protecting & Scaling Vacuums

My obsession with market vacuums began accidentally. I was tracking failed startups, trying to understand why brilliant ideas crash and burn, when a surprising insight emerged. It wasn't about the initial spark of innovation – it was about what happened after that first breakthrough.

The most enduring vacuum successes didn't stop at market entry; they methodically built moats around their positions through strategic barriers, customer lock-in, and calculated expansion into adjacent spaces. This revelation fundamentally changed how I understood vacuum creation.

This chapter delves into critical strategies and tactics, distilling the patterns I observed into actionable insights for protecting and scaling market vacuums. Through research and real-world examples, I've identified three key elements that successful vacuum creators consistently master:

1. ***Building Vacuum Barriers:*** Establishing robust defenses to prevent competitors from encroaching onto your market

position. This includes leveraging intellectual property, and creating network effects

2. ***Creating Switching Costs:*** Designing your product, service, and business model in a way that makes it increasingly difficult for customers to leave and choose alternative solutions. By building loyalty, ecosystem lock-in, and path dependencies, you can cement your leadership.

3. ***Expanding into Adjacent Vacuums:*** Strategically identifying and filling related market spaces to create a web of interconnected vacuums. This allows you to leverage your core capabilities, brand equity, and customer relationships to unlock new growth opportunities.

Let's dive into the first section.

1. Building Vacuum Barriers to Entry

The foundation of successful vacuum protection lies in establishing formidable barriers to entry. As the market leader, you must make it increasingly difficult for competitors to encroach on your hard-won position and erode your competitive advantages. This requires a multi-faceted approach that leverages intellectual property, network effects, and engineered switching costs.

Leveraging Intellectual Property

One of the primary ways to defend your vacuum is through the strategic use of intellectual property (IP). By securing patents, copyrights, and trademarks, you can create a legal moat around your innovative solutions, making it challenging for rivals to replicate your core functionality and features.

Patents, for instance, provide you with the exclusive right to prevent others from making, using, or selling your invention for a specified period, typically 20 years. This allows you to protect the technical underpinnings of your vacuum-filling solution, deterring competitors from simply copying your approach. Copyrights, on the other hand, safeguard the original expression of your ideas, such as the user interface design or the source code powering your platform.

Beyond traditional IP protection, successful vacuum fillers also explore more nuanced approaches to shielding their innovations. This may include developing trade secrets around proprietary algorithms, manufacturing processes, or business models. By keeping these critical elements closely guarded, you can make it prohibitively difficult and costly for rivals to catch up, even if they have access to your publicly available products or services.

Exclusive licensing agreements with key partners and suppliers can also strengthen your IP-based defenses. By locking in critical components, technologies, or distribution channels, you can effectively deny competitors the access they need to replicate your value proposition. This tactic has been employed extensively by companies like Apple, who have forged tight partnerships with component manufacturers and mobile network operators to cement their market dominance.

The overarching objective is to create a layered IP defense that not only protects your core offerings but also makes it increasingly arduous for rivals to overcome the legal and technical barriers you've erected. This IP-driven approach serves as a formidable first line of defense against encroaching competitors.

Cultivating Network Effects

Another powerful barrier to entry lies in the creation of robust network effects. By designing your solution to become more valuable as more users engage with it, you can trigger a self-reinforcing cycle of growth that leaves competitors struggling to gain traction.

Network effects occur when the value of a product or service increases as more people use it. This phenomenon can manifest in various ways, such as:

- Direct network effects: As more users join a messaging platform like WhatsApp, the value of the service increases for everyone, as they can communicate with a larger network of contacts.

- Indirect network effects: When a platform like Android or iOS attracts more app developers, the resulting growth in available apps makes the platform more attractive to end-users, further driving developer interest.

- Cross-side network effects: In a two-sided marketplace like Airbnb or Uber, the presence of more buyers (guests or riders) increases the value for sellers (hosts or drivers), and vice versa.

By intentionally designing your solution to harness these network effects, you can create a virtuous cycle of growth that becomes increasingly difficult for competitors to disrupt. As more users join your platform, the inherent value of your offering grows, making it more appealing to new users and further accelerating adoption.

The classic example is PayPal's dominance in the digital payments space. As more merchants and consumers adopted the platform, the network effects became increasingly pronounced - the larger the user base, the more valuable the service became for everyone involved. This made it exponentially harder for alternative payment solutions to displace PayPal's market position.

Successful vacuum fillers engineer network effects through a variety of mechanisms, such as:

- Building multi-sided platforms that connect customers, suppliers, and complementary service providers

- Incentivizing users to invite their networks to join the ecosystem, amplifying the user base

- Developing data-driven recommendation and personalization algorithms that improve with scale

- Integrating with third-party applications and services to expand the ecosystem's reach and utility

By systematically designing and nurturing these network effects, you can create a powerful barrier that deters competitors and solidifies your position as the go-to solution in the market.

2. Creating Switching Costs

Perhaps one of the most effective ways to protect your vacuum is by making it increasingly difficult for customers to switch to alternative offerings. By engineering high switching costs, you can lock in your user base and discourage them from defecting to rival solutions, even if those competitors offer similar or superior functionality.

Ways to Engineer High Switching Costs

Switching costs refer to the time, effort, and resources that a customer must invest in transitioning from one product or service to another. The higher these costs, the more reluctant customers will be to abandon your solution in favor of a competitor's offering.

Successful market creators build switching costs through a variety of strategies, such as:

1. Integration into core workflows: By deeply integrating your solution into the customer's business processes, daily routines, or essential software ecosystems, you create a high degree of operational dependence that makes it disruptive and costly to switch.

2. Bundled services and ecosystems: Offering a comprehensive suite of interconnected products and services, each with its own lock-in mechanisms, increases the overall switching costs for customers. This is a key tactic employed by companies like Microsoft, Apple, and Amazon.

3. Loyalty programs and subscription models: Reward-based loyalty programs and subscription-based pricing structures incentivize customers to remain loyal, as the sunk costs and foregone benefits of switching can be substantial.

4. Data portability and migration challenges: If moving to a competitor's solution requires extensive data migration, retraining, or the loss of historical records, you create significant friction that discourages customers from leaving.

5. Unique features and complementary offerings: By providing value-added services, features, or integrations that are exclusive

to your solution, you make it harder for customers to find a suitable replacement that can deliver the same level of functionality and convenience.

The objective of engineering high switching costs is to create an environment where the effort, cost, and disruption associated with switching outweigh the potential benefits of exploring alternative options. This locks customers into your vacuum and makes it exponentially harder for competitors to poach your user base.

By engineering high switching costs, you can cement your leadership position and discourage customers from defecting to rival offerings, even if those competitors match or exceed your core functionality.

Building Customer Loyalty

At the heart of high switching costs lies the cultivation of deep customer loyalty. By designing experiences that foster emotional connections, create habit-forming behaviors, and generate a sense of belonging, you can transform your customers from passive users into ardent advocates.

One powerful tactic is the deployment of reward-based loyalty programs. These programs, exemplified by initiatives like Amazon Prime, Apple's App Store points, and airline frequent flyer miles, incentivize customers to remain engaged and invested in your solution. The accrual of points, discounts, and exclusive benefits creates a compelling reason for customers to consolidate their spending and activities within your ecosystem, rather than spreading them across multiple providers.

Beyond mere transactional rewards, successful vacuum fillers also cultivate loyalty through personalized experiences and tailored recommendations. By leveraging customer data and advanced analytics, you can deliver increasingly relevant and valuable insights, products, and services that become deeply embedded in the customer's daily routines and decision-making processes. This personalization not only enhances the perceived value of your offering but also makes it more psychologically challenging for customers to abandon something so closely aligned with their individual needs and preferences.

Furthermore, the incorporation of social elements and community-building features can foster a sense of belonging that transcends the mere functional utility of your solution. Features like discussion forums, user-generated content, and shared achievements create a social fabric that customers are reluctant to leave, as doing so would mean severing ties with their trusted networks and communities.

Ecosystem Lock-in

Complementing the loyalty-building strategies, successful market creators also engineer their offerings to lock customers into an interconnected ecosystem of products and services. By creating robust integrations, data synergies, and platform-level interdependencies, you can make it prohibitively difficult for customers to extract themselves from your ecosystem and migrate to alternative solutions.

Consider the ecosystem lock-in strategies employed by tech giants like Apple and Google. Both companies have intentionally designed their mobile operating systems, digital content stores, productivity suites, and a myriad of other services to seamlessly integrate with one another. This means that customers who have invested time, money, and effort into building their digital lives within these ecosystems face significant hurdles in transitioning to competing platforms, as doing so would require the arduous process of migrating data, relearning workflows, and potentially forfeiting valuable digital assets.

Moreover, successful market creators often leverage the power of network effects to amplify their ecosystem lock-in capabilities. By creating multi-sided platforms that connect customers, suppliers, and complementary service providers, they can cultivate powerful feedback loops where the value of the ecosystem grows exponentially with each new participant. This makes it increasingly difficult for customers to leave, as the utility and convenience of the integrated services become indispensable to their daily activities and business operations.

Establishing Path Dependencies

In addition to cultivating loyalty and ecosystem lock-in, savvy companies also engineer path dependencies that make it arduous for customers to switch to alternative solutions, even if those competitors offer superior functionality or pricing.

Path dependencies arise when customers' past decisions, investments, and behavioral patterns create inertia that makes it difficult to change course. Successful companies leverage this principle by designing their solutions to become deeply embedded in the customer's workflows, habits, and decision-making frameworks.

This can be achieved through a variety of tactics, such as:

1. Integrating your solution into mission-critical business processes, where disrupting the status quo would incur significant operational and financial costs.

2. Establishing data-driven personalization and recommendation systems that become indispensable to the customer's daily decision-making.

3. Developing proprietary file formats, APIs, or other technical standards that make it challenging to migrate data and functionality to competing platforms.

4. Investing in extensive user training, custom configurations, and specialized skill development that are specific to your solution, creating a high relearning barrier.

5. Offering unique features, content, or access to resources that are only available through your ecosystem, making it difficult to replicate the same value proposition elsewhere.

By systematically engineering these path dependencies, you create a self-reinforcing cycle where the more deeply customers integrate your solution into their lives and workflows, the more difficult it becomes for them to contemplate switching to an alternative. This locks customers into your vacuum, further strengthening your market dominance.

The Power of Compounding in Switching Costs

The true power of switching cost engineering lies in the compounding effect of these various strategies. By layering loyalty-building, ecosystem lock-in, and path dependency mechanisms, you create a multifaceted web of interconnected barriers that makes it exponentially harder for customers to leave your solution.

As customers become more deeply embedded in your ecosystem, the overall switching costs they face increase exponentially. The time, effort, and disruption required to extract themselves from your integrated services, migrate their data and workflows, and rebuild their digital lives elsewhere becomes a formidable deterrent, even if a competitor offers a superior or more cost-effective alternative.

This compounding effect is a hallmark of market leaders who have mastered the art of vacuum protection and scaling. Companies like Apple, Amazon, and Microsoft have systematically designed their offerings to create this switching cost mosaic, cementing their position as indispensable partners for both individual consumers and enterprise customers.

3. Expanding into Adjacent Market Vacuums

Having established a strong defensive position around your core market vacuum, the next step in your growth strategy is to strategically expand into related market spaces. By identifying and filling adjacent vacuums, you can leverage your core capabilities, brand equity, and customer relationships to unlock new opportunities and cement your position as the dominant player in the broader industry landscape.

The key to successful adjacent vacuum expansion lies in a methodical, well-planned approach. This is not about haphazardly diversifying into unrelated domains; rather, it's a systematic process of identifying and capturing nearby vacuums that amplify the value of your existing offerings and ecosystem.

Apple's ecosystem expansion provides a prime example of this strategy in action. Starting with the revolutionary iPhone, the company has systematically filled adjacent vacuums in mobile computing, digital content, and financial services. By creating a tightly integrated ecosystem of products and services, Apple was able to not only defend its smartphone dominance but also unlock new revenue streams and solidify its status as a leading technology conglomerate.

When evaluating potential adjacent vacuums to fill, successful vacuum timers consider several key factors:

Synergies with Core Capabilities

The first critical element is understanding how you can leverage your existing technical expertise, operational know-how, and brand reputation to deliver unique value in the new market space. What core strengths can you bring to bear, and how do they align with the unmet needs of the adjacent vacuum?

For instance, when Amazon expanded into cloud computing with AWS, they were able to draw upon their deep experience in large-scale infrastructure management, data center operations, and software development. This allowed them to create a cloud platform that was tailored to the specific requirements of enterprise customers, setting them apart from traditional IT service providers.

Ecosystem Reinforcement

Beyond just unlocking new revenue streams, the successful expansion into adjacent vacuums should also strengthen and expand your existing ecosystem. By creating tighter integration and synergies between your offerings, you can make the overall value proposition more compelling for customers, increasing the barriers to exit and amplifying the network effects that underpin your market dominance.

Apple's seamless integration of the iPhone, iPad, Mac, and a suite of digital services is a prime example of this principle in action. Each new device or service added to the ecosystem increases the switching costs for customers, as they become more dependent on the interconnected nature of the Apple universe.

Switching Cost Amplification

Directly related to ecosystem reinforcement is the concept of amplifying switching costs. By carefully designing how your adjacent vacuum-filling initiatives intersect with your core offerings, you can make it even harder for customers to contemplate leaving your ecosystem in favor of competing solutions.

This could involve deeply integrating new products and services, creating data portability challenges, or offering bundled pricing and subscription models that make it prohibitively expensive and disruptive for customers to extract themselves from your web of offerings. The objective is to create a self-reinforcing cycle where each new vacuum you fill increases the overall switching costs for your customers.

Growth Potential

Of course, the identification and selection of adjacent vacuums must also be guided by a clear-eyed assessment of the market opportunity and growth potential. What is the size and trajectory of the adjacent market, and how does it align with your strategic ambitions and financial goals? Are there sufficient untapped customers and unmet needs to justify the investment required to enter and scale in the new space?

Careful analysis of factors like market size, growth rates, competitive intensity, and customer willingness to pay can help you prioritize the most promising adjacent vacuums and allocate resources accordingly. This ensures that your expansion efforts not only strengthen your core business but also unlock meaningful new avenues for sustainable, long-term growth.

Competitive Dynamics

Finally, successful vacuum creators also carefully consider the competitive landscape and timing of their adjacent vacuum initiatives. By strategically entering new market spaces before rivals can effectively respond, you can establish a dominant position and erect high barriers to entry that make it exponentially harder for competitors to challenge your supremacy.

Apple's methodical rollout of the iPad, for instance, allowed the company to carve out a leadership position in the emerging tablet computing market before Microsoft, Google, and others could mount a credible response. This early mover advantage, combined with the ecosystem integration and switching cost amplification tactics, has helped Apple maintain its dominance in the tablet space for over a decade.

By applying this multi-faceted lens to adjacent vacuum identification and expansion, leading companies transform their initial vacuum-filling success into a sprawling web of interconnected market spaces. Each new initiative not only generates additional revenue and profit but also strengthens the defensibility of the overall ecosystem, making it increasingly difficult for competitors to chip away at your hard-won market position.

Real-World Examples of Vacuum Protection and Scaling

As we've explored in the previous sections, the journey of creating a successful vacuum-filling solution doesn't end with the initial market entry. The true test of market leadership lies in a company's ability to erect formidable barriers to entry, engineer high switching costs, and strategically expand into adjacent market spaces. By mastering these critical strategies, vacuum timers can transform their initial success into enduring dominance.

To bring these principles to life, let's examine how several leading companies across diverse industries have executed on the imperatives of vacuum protection and scaling.

Shopify's Platform Vacuum: Engineering the Future of Commerce

Shopify's approach to vacuum protection and scaling demonstrates how modern platforms can create formidable barriers to entry while continuously expanding their ecosystem. When Shopify emerged in 2006, it didn't just create an e-commerce platform - it engineered an entire business operating system for merchants that would become increasingly indispensable over time.

The foundation of Shopify's vacuum protection strategy begins with deep platform integration. Rather than simply providing online storefronts, Shopify systematically embedded itself into every aspect of a merchant's business operations:

1. Technical Infrastructure Lock-in

At first glance, Shopify's technical infrastructure might appear simply as a collection of e-commerce tools. However, the company has masterfully engineered a sophisticated digital foundation that becomes deeply woven into a merchant's business operations. Like the roots of a tree that grows deeper and more intertwined over time, Shopify's technical infrastructure creates an increasingly strong foundation that becomes challenging to uproot.

This infrastructure lock-in begins with the seemingly basic elements of e-commerce:

- Custom domain and hosting infrastructure that becomes the merchant's digital storefront and brand identity online

- Integrated payment processing through Shopify Payments that handles not just transactions but also complex aspects like fraud prevention, international currencies, and payment reconciliation

- Customized themes and store design that merchants invest time and resources to perfect their brand experience

- Complex inventory management systems that track products across multiple sales channels and locations

- Order fulfillment workflows that coordinate everything from customer communications to shipping logistics

What makes this infrastructure particularly powerful is how each element reinforces the others. A merchant's custom theme isn't just about aesthetics – it's integrated with their inventory system, which connects to their fulfillment workflow, which ties into their payment processing. Over time, as merchants build their operations on these technical foundations, the prospect of migrating to another platform becomes increasingly daunting. Each customization they make, each integration they set up, and each data point they accumulate adds another thread to the fabric that binds them to the platform.

2. Ecosystem Expansion

If technical infrastructure represents the roots of Shopify's strategy, their ecosystem expansion exemplifies the branches reaching into every aspect of modern commerce. Rather than remaining content as a simple e-commerce platform, Shopify has systematically identified and filled critical gaps in merchants' business needs, creating what could be called a "commerce operating system."

This expansion flows naturally from merchants' evolving needs:

- Shopify POS elegantly bridges the digital-physical divide, transforming scattered retail operations into a unified commerce experience

- Shopify Capital solves the age-old challenge of business financing by leveraging real-time sales data to offer precisely timed funding

- Shopify Shipping turns logistics from a headache into a competitive advantage through negotiated rates and integrated fulfillment

- Shopify Markets removes the complexity of international expansion, handling everything from currency conversion to local regulations

- Shop Pay elevates the payment experience from a transaction to a seamless commerce identity for consumers

What makes this ecosystem expansion particularly powerful is its organic nature. Each new service doesn't just solve a problem – it creates synergies with existing solutions. When merchants adopt Shopify Capital, for instance, they gain not just financing but optimized cash flow predictions based on their POS data. When they use Shopify Shipping, they're not just getting discounted rates but integrated inventory management across all sales channels.

3. Network Effect Engineering

Perhaps Shopify's most sophisticated achievement lies in how it has engineered multiple, reinforcing network effects that transform the platform from a service provider into an indispensable commerce utility. Like a digital bazaar that becomes more valuable with each new merchant and customer, Shopify has created a virtuous cycle of growing value.

This network effect manifests in several powerful ways:

- The App Marketplace functions as a vibrant innovation ecosystem where third-party developers continuously create new capabilities, making the platform more valuable for all merchants

- Shop Pay's growing consumer adoption creates a network of trusted buyers, increasing conversion rates for all Shopify merchants

- The Fulfillment Network becomes more efficient and cost-effective as more merchants join, creating shared economies of scale

- The Shop app transforms independent stores into a connected commerce network, where each new merchant adds to the discovery potential for all

These network effects are particularly powerful because they're multi-sided and self-reinforcing. When more developers join the ecosystem, they create better tools, which attract more merchants, which draw more developers. As more consumers use Shop Pay, conversion rates improve, attracting more merchants, leading to wider Shop Pay adoption.

4. Data Moat Building

In the modern commerce landscape, data isn't just a byproduct of operations – it's a strategic asset that becomes more valuable over time. Shopify has masterfully turned its scale into a unique competitive advantage by creating what we might call a "data flywheel" that continuously deepens its defensive moat.

This data advantage manifests across multiple dimensions:

- Transaction data across millions of merchants reveals deep insights into consumer behavior and market trends

- Consumer purchasing patterns enable increasingly sophisticated recommendation engines

- Inventory and supply chain data helps optimize operations and predict market demands

- Marketing performance metrics guide merchants toward more effective strategies

- Sales trend analysis enables more accurate business forecasting and planning

What makes this data moat particularly powerful is its compound effect. Each transaction, each customer interaction, each inventory adjustment adds to a growing pool of insights that makes Shopify's platform progressively smarter. This intelligence then translates into better merchant tools, leading to more successful businesses, generating more valuable data.

5. Innovation Acceleration

In the fast-paced world of digital commerce, standing still means falling behind. Shopify has transformed this challenge into a strategic advantage by positioning itself not just as a platform but as an innovation partner for its merchants. Like a technological lighthouse, Shopify illuminates new opportunities and guides merchants through evolving commerce landscapes.

This innovation-first approach manifests across multiple frontiers:

- Mobile commerce optimization that turned smartphones from browsing devices into conversion engines

- Augmented reality tools that bring products to life in customers' spaces before purchase

- Cryptocurrency payment integration that opens merchants to new customer segments and payment methods

- NFT-enabled commerce that creates unique digital ownership opportunities

- Social commerce connections that turn social media from marketing channels into direct sales platforms

What makes Shopify's innovation strategy particularly powerful is its risk-reduction effect for merchants. Rather than betting individually on emerging technologies, merchants can rely on Shopify's carefully curated and tested innovations. When a new commerce trend emerges, merchants know they'll have access to battle-tested solutions through their existing platform.

The Impact of Shopify's Strategy

The true measure of a vacuum protection strategy lies not in its theoretical elegance but in its practical results. Shopify's approach has created what we might call a "prosperity flywheel" – where merchant success reinforces platform strength, which enables more merchant success.

This impact manifests in several key metrics:

- Merchant retention rates that significantly exceed industry standards

- Consistent growth in Gross Merchandise Volume, indicating healthy merchant businesses

- Expanding revenue per merchant as businesses adopt more platform services

- A thriving ecosystem of third-party developers continuously adding platform value

- Accelerating adoption of additional services by existing merchants

But perhaps more telling than these metrics is the qualitative transformation Shopify has achieved. They've created what we might call a "compounding vacuum" – one that becomes stronger over time through multiple reinforcing mechanisms:

- Each new merchant makes the platform more valuable for others through shared insights

- Each new service increases switching costs and platform utility

- Each new integration deepens the moat around their market position

- Each new data point makes their insights more valuable

- Each new innovation makes their platform more indispensable

Modern Lessons in Vacuum Protection

Shopify's sophisticated approach to vacuum protection offers crucial lessons for modern business leaders:

1. *Integration Depth:* Success lies not in creating surface-level switching costs but in becoming deeply embedded in core business operations. The goal isn't to make switching inconvenient but to make it nearly unthinkable because of the value provided.

2. *Ecosystem Thinking:* True defensibility comes from building interconnected systems where each element multiplies the value of others. It's about creating not just products but entire business environments that grow more valuable over time.

3. *Network Effect Engineering:* Sustainable competitive advantages emerge from designing systems where growth naturally creates

increasing returns and rising barriers to competition. The key is to make your platform more valuable with each new participant.

4. *Data Advantage Creation:* In the modern economy, data isn't just a byproduct – it's a strategic asset that compounds in value over time. The goal is to create unique insights that become self-reinforcing competitive advantages.

5. *Innovation Leadership:* Long-term success requires staying ahead of market trends to ensure customers never need to look elsewhere for emerging capabilities. It's about making innovation a systematic rather than occasional process.

The Future Implications

Shopify's example suggests that future vacuum protection will rely less on traditional barriers and more on creating expanding spheres of value that become increasingly difficult to replicate. Success will come not from defending territory but from continuously expanding capabilities in ways that create natural competitive insulation.

To me, this modern approach to vacuum protection represents a shift from defensive thinking to value creation at scale. It suggests that the best protection comes not from building walls but from creating so much value that leaving becomes unthinkable. As markets continue to evolve, this approach to vacuum protection – based on continuous innovation and expanding value creation – will likely become even more crucial for sustainable competitive advantage.

The Cognitive Frameworks of Market Creators

Chapter 7

Seven Distinctive Mindsets of Vacuum Creators

What began as research into market vacuums - those invisible spaces of opportunity that reshape industries - led me down a fascinating path of studying the minds behind these innovations. I realized that understanding the principles of market creation wasn't enough; I needed to understand the people who consistently spotted them.

Along with studying the likes of Steve Jobs and Walt Disney - whose stories we know well - I also spent time studying lesser-known innovators: small-scale entrepreneurs who transformed local industries, quiet inventors whose products we use daily but whose names we never learned, and business leaders in emerging markets who solved problems in ways Silicon Valley never imagined.

A pattern began to emerge from these diverse stories. These vacuum creators, regardless of their scale or sector, seemed to perceive reality through distinctive lenses that fundamentally altered how they saw opportunities. It wasn't just about being creative or strategic - they had developed sophisticated mental operating systems that enabled them to spot invisible spaces that others overlooked.

I remember sitting in my study one evening, surrounded by interview transcripts and case studies, when it hit me: these weren't just personality traits or learned behaviors. These were systematic ways of processing reality that could be identified, understood, and potentially cultivated. The entrepreneurs I studied weren't born with special abilities - they had developed specific mindsets that transformed how they saw the world.

After analyzing hundreds of cases and conducting dozens of interviews, I identified seven distinct mindsets that consistently appeared among successful vacuum creators. From intersectional curiosity that connected seemingly unrelated dots to legacy consciousness that built institutions spanning generations, these mindsets formed a sophisticated toolkit for identifying and seizing opportunities.

In this chapter, we'll explore these seven mindsets in detail. Understanding them isn't just about self-improvement - it's about acquiring new lenses through which to spot the hidden opportunities that others overlook. My hope is that by sharing these insights, I can help you develop the same sophisticated mental models that enabled history's greatest innovators to see what others couldn't.

The journey to uncover these mindsets taught me something profound: the ability to spot market vacuums isn't a gift bestowed upon a chosen few. It's a capability that can be developed by understanding and cultivating specific ways of thinking. Let's explore how.

Seven Distinctive Mindsets
of Vacuum Creators

(1) Intersectional Curiosity
Connecting dots across unrelated domains

(2) Temporal Arbitrage
Bridging present and future opportunities

(3) Systemic Simplification
Making complexity feel effortlessly simple

(4) Reverse Status Quo
Challenging fundamental market assumptions

(5) Trust Orchestration
Systematically building networks of confidence

(6) Scale Paradox Mastery
Maintaining intimacy while scaling massively

(7) Legacy Consciousness
Designing for generational impact

Mindset 1 - The Art of Intersectional Curiosity

History's greatest vacuum creators share a distinctive cognitive trait that extends far beyond conventional business acumen – what we might call "intersectional curiosity." This isn't merely about being interested in multiple fields; it's about developing an almost anthropological ability to spot hidden patterns and connections across seemingly unrelated domains.

Understanding Intersectional Curiosity

This mindset manifests in three key dimensions, each illuminating a different facet of how great vacuum creators think across boundaries.

1. Cross-Domain Pattern Recognition

Consider Steve Jobs' famous fascination with calligraphy. While studying these ancient letterforms at Reed College, Jobs wasn't merely appreciating their aesthetic beauty. He was unconsciously building a mental framework about how humans interact with visual information – insights that would later revolutionize digital typography and user interface design.

The significance of this pattern recognition went far beyond mere aesthetic appreciation. Jobs was developing a deep understanding of how visual forms communicate meaning, how spacing affects readability, and how subtle variations in shape can convey different emotional tones. These insights weren't confined to calligraphy – they became fundamental principles in how Apple approached all aspects of human-computer interaction.

When the Macintosh debuted with its revolutionary typography, it wasn't just about having beautiful fonts. It represented a fundamental understanding of how humans process and engage with visual information. Jobs had translated the timeless principles of calligraphic artistry into the digital age, creating an entirely new standard for how computers could communicate with users.

2. Cultural-Commercial Integration

Phil Knight, the co-founder of Nike (originally Blue Ribbon Sports), exemplifies a different facet of intersectional curiosity. A Stanford graduate and former runner who transformed a small shoe distribution business into a global athletic brand, Knight saw beyond conventional sportswear marketing. While most sportswear executives saw athletic equipment as mere products, Knight's curiosity about athlete psychology and cultural movements led him to spot unique patterns in how sports gear could become a form of personal expression and social identity.

The Air Jordan project illustrates this integration perfectly. It emerged not from traditional market research but from Knight's keen observation of Michael Jordan's transformative impact on basketball and popular culture. Where others saw a basketball player, Knight recognized a pattern that connected athletic performance, personal branding, and cultural aspiration. His curiosity about social dynamics helped him spot a vacuum that traditional sports marketing had missed.

This wasn't just about creating a signature shoe line. It was about understanding how athletic equipment intersects with personal identity, cultural inspiration, and social empowerment. The Air Jordan represented a synthesis of design innovation, athletic achievement, and cultural storytelling – a combination that could only emerge from deep curiosity about how different systems interact.

3. Synthesis of Disparate Elements

Walt Disney's intersectional curiosity led him to blend animation, storytelling, architecture, and crowd psychology in unprecedented ways. His theme parks weren't just entertainment venues; they represented a sophisticated synthesis of how people move through spaces, how stories create emotional engagement, and how different sensory experiences combine to create immersion.

Disney's genius lay in his ability to see connections between seemingly unrelated fields. He understood that the principles of animation – timing, pacing, emotional build-up – could apply equally to how people experience physical spaces. The design of Main Street USA wasn't just about creating a nostalgic atmosphere; it reflected deep insights into human psychology, social interaction, and narrative structure.

This synthesis went far beyond superficial combination. Disney created experiences that wove together spatial design, storytelling, and human behavior in ways that seemed natural and inevitable once executed but required remarkable intersectional thinking to conceive.

Intersectional Curiosity

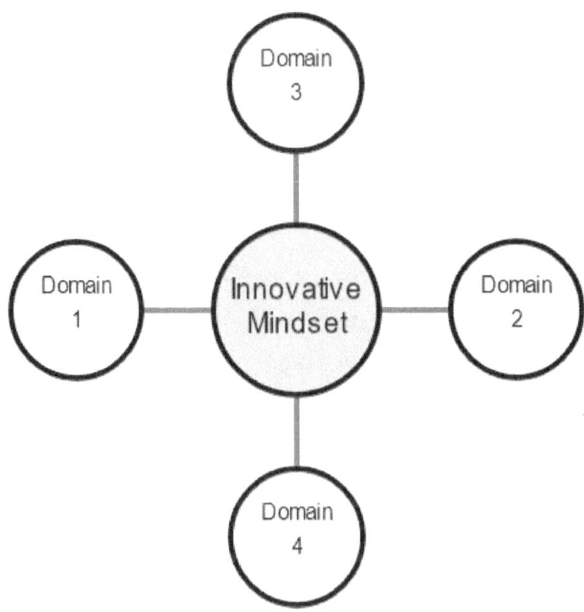

Cultivating Intersectional Curiosity

The development of this mindset requires systematic cultivation of three fundamental practices:

1. **Active Cross Pollination**

   True intersectional curiosity begins with deliberate exposure to diverse fields of knowledge. This isn't about casual browsing or superficial sampling. It requires deep engagement with multiple domains, seeking not just information but understanding of fundamental principles.

   Successful vacuum creators approach this through systematic study across disciplines. They read deeply in fields far from their primary expertise. They engage with diverse expert communities, not as a networking exercise but as a way to understand different modes of thinking. They actively collect experiences outside their comfort zones, using each new exposure as an opportunity to spot patterns and connections.

2. **Pattern Documentation**

   The power of intersectional curiosity lies not just in exposure to different domains, but in actively connecting insights across fields. This requires systematic documentation and reflection on the patterns one observes.

   Great vacuum creators maintain detailed journals of their observations and insights. They create maps showing connections between different domains, actively looking for principles that translate across fields. Most importantly, they regularly reflect on these connections, allowing insights to emerge from the juxtaposition of seemingly unrelated observations.

3. Experimental Synthesis

The final practice involves actively testing cross-domain insights through practical experimentation. This means moving beyond theoretical connections to actual implementation, even if only in prototype form.

Successful practitioners regularly test combinations of unrelated concepts, seeking feedback from diverse audiences. They prototype ideas that blend different fields, using each experiment as an opportunity to refine their understanding of how different domains can interact and create value.

Impact on Vacuum Creation

The power of intersectional curiosity in vacuum creation manifests in three crucial ways:

First, it enables the identification of hidden vacuums that others miss. By understanding patterns across multiple domains, these innovators can spot opportunities that exist not within traditional industry boundaries but at the convergence of different fields. They see connections that others overlook precisely because they're looking through multiple lenses simultaneously.

Second, it enables the engineering of novel solutions by importing insights from one domain to solve problems in another. This cross-pollination of ideas often leads to breakthrough innovations that would be impossible to conceive from within a single field of expertise.

Finally, it creates sustainable competitive advantages that are difficult to replicate. Solutions born from intersectional insights often require deep understanding of multiple domains to appreciate fully, making them naturally resistant to simple imitation.

The art of intersectional curiosity thus becomes not just a personal characteristic but a powerful tool for identifying and creating new market spaces. It enables vacuum creators to see opportunities that others miss and to craft solutions that others would find difficult to conceive or copy.

Mindset 2 - Temporal Arbitrage: Dancing Between Now and Next

The most profound market opportunities exist not in the present or future alone, but in the delicate dance between timeframes. While most business leaders focus on either immediate market needs or future predictions, vacuum creators possess an almost orchestral ability to conduct business across multiple time horizons simultaneously. This isn't merely about long-term thinking – it's about actively creating value in the present while systematically building bridges to inevitable futures.

Understanding Temporal Arbitrage

This sophisticated mindset manifests in three distinct dimensions, each revealing a different aspect of how great vacuum creators navigate time.

1. **Present-Future Bridge Building**

   Consider Elon Musk's approach with Tesla. While the automotive industry viewed electric vehicles through a binary lens – seeing only the present limitations (expensive, limited range) or distant future possibilities (affordable, practical) – Musk orchestrated a masterful progression that bridged these timeframes.

The Roadster, Tesla's first vehicle, exemplifies this bridge-building mindset. On the surface, it was a high-end sports car targeting wealthy early adopters. But this was merely the visible element of a deeper strategy. Each Roadster sold was simultaneously serving multiple temporal purposes: generating current revenue, funding technology development, building brand prestige, and most importantly, creating the stepping stones that would make mass-market electric vehicles inevitable.

Musk understood that the path to affordable electric cars couldn't be achieved by directly attacking the mass market. Instead, he crafted a temporal bridge: using high-margin luxury vehicles to fund the development of increasingly accessible models. Each product wasn't just a car; it was a carefully calculated step in a longer journey, simultaneously serving present needs while building future capabilities.

2. Strategic Patience with Tactical Urgency

Jeff Bezos's approach at Amazon provides perhaps the clearest illustration of this dimension. His famous letter to shareholders declaring it would always be "Day 1" at Amazon wasn't just a catchy slogan – it represented a sophisticated understanding of temporal dynamics in business.

While patiently building infrastructure for a digital future few could imagine, Bezos simultaneously demonstrated relentless urgency in improving present customer experience. This wasn't contradictory; it was a carefully orchestrated balance. The development of AWS perfectly exemplifies this mindset. While the cloud computing service wasn't born from immediate market demand, it emerged from Bezos's recognition that Amazon's internal needs today would become tomorrow's market opportunities.

The genius lay in how AWS was developed. Rather than building it as a speculative future project, Amazon created it to solve their own immediate needs. This meant the infrastructure was battle-tested by real usage while the market was still maturing. By the time external customers were ready for cloud services, Amazon had already developed robust capabilities and deep understanding of the challenges involved.

3. Inevitable Future Exploitation

Marc Andreessen's (co-founder of Netscape and influential venture capitalist) approach to digital communication and internet technology demonstrates perhaps the most sophisticated application of temporal arbitrage. When other technologists were viewing the internet as a niche academic network, Andreessen focused on what he saw as inevitable: the transformation of global communication and information access through web browsers.

This wasn't just strategic foresight; it was a deep understanding of how to create value across time horizons. While web browsers were initially a crude technological experiment, the need for intuitive digital interfaces was inevitable. By developing Mosaic and then Netscape, Andreessen created immediate value through technological innovation while positioning himself to benefit from the fundamental redesign of how humans interact with information.

His approach shows how temporal arbitrage masters identify and exploit inevitable futures. They don't try to predict every detail of the future; instead, they identify elements that must exist in any future scenario and build positions around those certainties. Andreessen's early investments in web technologies and later in transformative digital platforms represent a systematic approach to capturing value from what he perceived as unavoidable technological and communication shifts

Temporal Arbitrage

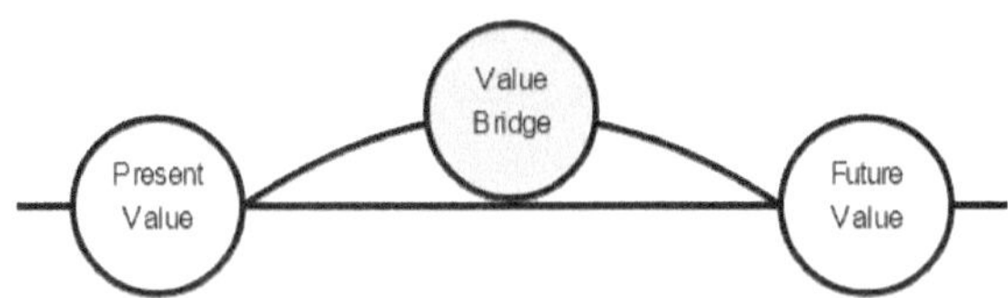

The Practice of Temporal Arbitrage

The development and application of this mindset involves three fundamental practices, each requiring systematic cultivation and conscious application.

1. Future Pattern Recognition

The first practice involves developing the ability to distinguish between merely possible futures and truly inevitable ones. This isn't about crystal ball gazing or making wild predictions. Instead, it focuses on identifying patterns and trends that have unstoppable momentum.

This requires a deep understanding of how technologies evolve, how human behaviors change, and how social systems develop. Successful practitioners spend significant time studying the sequences of enabling technologies – understanding not just what might be possible, but what must happen first for those possibilities to materialize.

More importantly, they pay careful attention to social and behavioral shifts that have momentum. These changes, once started, tend to continue regardless of technological or market fluctuations. The shift toward digital payments, for instance, represents not just a technological trend but a fundamental change in human behavior that, once begun, was unlikely to reverse.

2. Present Value Creation

The second practice involves deliberately creating current value while building future capabilities. This isn't about choosing between now and later – it's about designing systems that serve both timeframes simultaneously.

This requires a sophisticated business model design that can evolve over time. Successful practitioners create flexible systems that can generate immediate revenue while developing capabilities that will be valuable in future scenarios. They focus on building assets that appreciate as their anticipated futures materialize, creating compound value across time.

3. Bridge Building

The third practice involves actively creating connections between present capabilities and future needs. This goes beyond simply preparing for the future; it involves actively shaping the path that leads there.

This includes developing technologies that can evolve over time, creating educational initiatives that prepare users for future solutions, and building infrastructure that can serve both current and future needs. The key is to create elements that have value today while maintaining the flexibility to adapt to emerging opportunities.

Impact on Vacuum Creation

The power of temporal arbitrage in vacuum creation manifests in three crucial ways:

First, it enables risk reduction in long-term investments. By creating present value while building future capabilities, these innovators can fund their journey toward larger opportunities. This makes ambitious projects sustainable where pure future bets would fail.

Second, it creates unique competitive advantages. The ability to operate effectively across multiple time horizons builds capabilities and positions that are extremely difficult for competitors to replicate. This temporal sophistication becomes a moat protecting market leadership.

Finally, it enables natural market leadership. By preparing for futures while delivering present value, temporal arbitrage practitioners position themselves as the obvious leaders in emerging opportunities. They don't just predict the future – they help shape it while building the capabilities needed to dominate it.

The art of temporal arbitrage thus becomes not just a strategic tool but a fundamental mindset for creating and capturing value across time. It enables vacuum creators to build sustainable paths to ambitious futures while creating value every step of the way.

Mindset 3 - Systemic Simplification

In a world obsessed with adding features and functionality, the true masters of vacuum creation possess an almost paradoxical ability: making complex systems appear effortlessly simple to users while building sophisticated infrastructures behind the scenes. This isn't mere minimalism; it's the art of abstracting complexity to create elegant, accessible solutions to intricate problems. The most profound innovations often appear deceptively simple on the surface, concealing layers of sophisticated engineering beneath a seamless user experience.

Understanding Systemic Simplification

This sophisticated mindset manifests in three key dimensions, each revealing a different aspect of how great vacuum creators approach complexity.

1. **Interface Elegance**

   Consider Dyson's founder James Dyson's revolutionary approach to vacuum cleaner design. While home appliance manufacturers typically competed on technical specifications, Dyson took the counterintuitive path of reimagining user experience. Behind the seemingly simple cyclonic suction technology lay an intricate maze of engineering challenges – airflow dynamics, particle separation, material innovations – yet users experienced none of this complexity. They simply used a vacuum that worked more effectively than anything they had encountered before.

The genius wasn't in solving these complex engineering problems, though that itself was a remarkable achievement. The true innovation lay in making all that complexity invisible to the user. Dyson understood that the most sophisticated technology should feel like magic – present but unseen, powerful but unobtrusive. This wasn't about showcasing technical prowess; it was about ensuring users never needed to understand the underlying technological mechanisms.

This approach represented a fundamental shift in thinking about home appliance design. While other manufacturers cluttered their products with multiple attachments and complicated settings, Dyson buried its technological complexity beneath a layer of apparent simplicity. The bagless, transparent design wasn't just an aesthetic choice; it was a philosophy about how technology could solve everyday problems with unprecedented elegance and ease.

2. Complexity Absorption

Steve Jobs exemplified this dimension through Apple's revolutionary product philosophy. The iPhone wasn't just a combination of existing devices – it was a complete reimagining of how humans could interact with technology. While it combined the functionalities of a phone, camera, computer, music player, and dozens of other devices, its interface made these capabilities accessible to a child.

Jobs understood that true innovation isn't about exposing complexity to users, but about absorbing it into the system. The achievement wasn't in the technical sophistication –

though that was considerable – but in its concealment. Every feature, every capability was carefully considered not just for its functionality, but for how it could be made intuitive and accessible.

This approach required a complete rethinking of human-computer interaction. Rather than expecting users to adapt to technology's complexity, Apple redesigned technology to match human intuition. The result wasn't just a simpler device; it was a new paradigm for how technology could serve human needs.

3. Essential Reduction

Jack Ma's development of Alipay demonstrates perhaps the most sophisticated application of systemic simplification in financial services. Rather than adding features to existing banking systems, Ma stripped financial transactions down to their essential elements, then rebuilt them for the digital age with radical simplicity at their core.

This wasn't about making banking slightly easier; it was about fundamentally reimagining what financial transactions could be. By reducing the essential elements of trust and transaction to their core, then rebuilding them with digital simplicity, Ma created a system whose complexity served to create simplicity, rather than showcase itself.

The genius lay in understanding that true simplification often requires deep sophistication. The simpler the user experience became, the more complex the underlying systems needed to be. Yet this complexity was never an end in itself – it existed solely to enable simplicity for the user.

Systemic Simplification

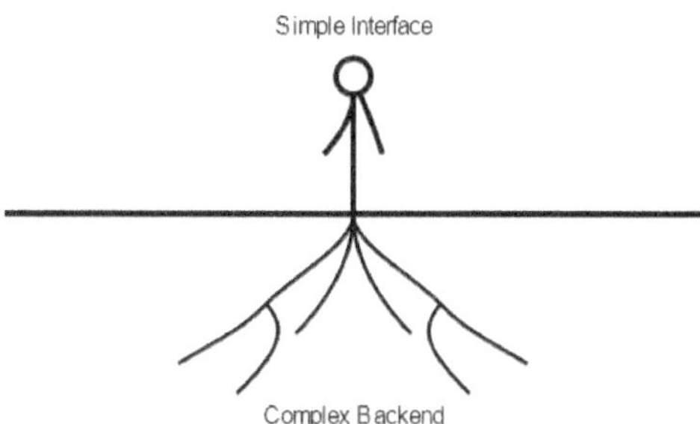

The Practice of Systemic Simplification

The development and application of this mindset involves three fundamental practices, each requiring systematic cultivation and conscious application.

1. **Complexity Mapping**

   The first step in systemic simplification is developing a deep understanding of the complexity you're trying to simplify. This isn't just about documenting features or functions; it's about understanding the fundamental nature of the problem you're solving.

   This requires careful analysis of user needs beneath feature requests. Often, what users ask for isn't what they truly need. By mapping the underlying needs and goals, you can identify which complexities are essential to the solution and which are merely accidental byproducts of current approaches.

   More importantly, this practice involves understanding system interdependencies – how different elements interact, what relationships are crucial, and which connections can be abstracted away. This deep understanding becomes the foundation for meaningful simplification.

2. Interface Distillation

The second practice involves the careful craft of reducing complex interactions to their simplest possible form. This isn't about removing features; it's about making them accessible through more elegant interfaces.

This requires sophisticated thinking about user interaction flows. How can complex tasks be broken down into intuitive steps? How can advanced features be progressively revealed as users need them? The goal is to create interfaces that feel natural and obvious, even when they're performing complex operations.

3. Infrastructure Sophistication

The third practice involves building the robust systems needed to support apparent simplicity. This is where the real complexity lives – in creating infrastructures sophisticated enough to make simplicity possible.

This includes developing scalable architectures that can handle growing demands without showing strain, building invisible safety nets that catch errors before users encounter them, and creating systems flexible enough to evolve without disrupting the simple user experience they enable.

Impact on Vacuum Creation

The power of systemic simplification in vacuum creation manifests in three crucial ways:

First, it enables rapid adoption of new solutions. By making complex capabilities accessible through simple interfaces, these innovations can spread far more quickly than their more complicated counterparts. The sophistication of the backend ensures this simplicity can scale.

Second, it creates powerful competitive moats. The gap between simple interfaces and the complex capabilities that enable them becomes a significant barrier to competition. While interfaces can be copied, the sophisticated systems behind them are much harder to replicate.

Finally, it builds deeper user trust. When systems work reliably and simply, users develop stronger confidence than they do with visibly complex systems. This trust becomes a crucial asset in maintaining market leadership.

Systemic simplification thus becomes not just a design philosophy but a fundamental approach to creating sustainable market advantages. It enables vacuum creators to make sophisticated innovations accessible to broad audiences while building defensible positions through the underlying complexity that enables that simplicity.

Mindset 4 - Reverse Status Quo

While most see boundaries as walls, vacuum creators see them as doors waiting to be opened. Their unique ability to question fundamental assumptions isn't mere contrarianism – it's a disciplined practice of reimagining reality by challenging what others accept as given. These innovators understand that the most profound opportunities often lie not in accepting industry constraints, but in systematically questioning why these constraints exist at all.

Understanding Reverse Status Quo

This transformative mindset manifests in three key dimensions, each revealing a different aspect of how great vacuum creators reimagine possibilities.

1. **Assumption Inversion**

   Consider Herb Kelleher's revolutionary approach at Southwest Airlines. When he looked at the airline industry in the late 1960s, he saw an operating model built on unquestioned assumptions that had calcified into "industry truths." Airlines assumed they needed to serve meals, provide assigned seating, operate different types of aircraft, and maintain complex hub-and-spoke networks. Most fundamentally, they assumed that you couldn't combine low costs with high employee satisfaction and strong customer service.

   Rather than accepting these premises, Kelleher systematically challenged each one. He asked radical questions: Why do passengers on short flights need meals? What if the absence of assigned seating could actually speed up turnaround times? Could an airline operate more efficiently with just one type of aircraft? Most importantly, what if happy employees were actually the key to low costs through increased productivity and reduced turnover?

The genius lay not in any single innovation but in Kelleher's systematic dismantling of industry assumptions. By questioning each "must have" element of traditional airline operations, he created an entirely new operating model that competitors found impossible to replicate. Southwest didn't just offer lower prices – it created a new category of air travel that transformed the entire industry.

2. Constraint Transformation

Ingvar Kamprad's work at IKEA exemplifies perhaps the most sophisticated application of constraint transformation in retail history. When others saw the limitations of furniture retail – high storage costs, expensive delivery, assembly challenges – Kamprad saw opportunities to reimagine the entire business model.

Instead of accepting these constraints as problems to be minimized, he transformed each one into a source of competitive advantage. The challenge of furniture assembly became a way to dramatically reduce costs. Storage limitations led to the innovation of flat-pack design. High retail space costs sparked the creation of warehouse showrooms that became retail destinations in themselves.

This wasn't just clever problem-solving; it was a fundamental reimagining of retail possibilities. Each apparent constraint became a building block for a new kind of retail experience. IKEA's genius lay in creating a system where each transformed limitation reinforced the others: flat-pack design enabled warehouse storage, which enabled self-service, which justified customer assembly, which allowed lower prices.

Most remarkably, Kamprad transformed what others saw as the ultimate constraint – customer unwillingness to assemble furniture – into a key feature of the IKEA experience. By making assembly part of the value proposition rather than a necessary evil, IKEA created a deeper connection between customers and their furniture.

3. Convention Disruption

Tony Hsieh's approach at Zappos demonstrates how questioning fundamental conventions can create entirely new market positions. While the entire call center industry optimized around call duration metrics, Hsieh asked a simple but profound question: Why are we measuring time instead of satisfaction?

This wasn't just about changing metrics – it was about reimagining the entire purpose of customer service. By eliminating time measurements entirely and focusing instead on customer satisfaction, Hsieh didn't just improve service quality; he created a new paradigm for what customer service could be. The traditional constraint of efficiency was replaced by the opportunity for genuine human connection.

This disruption rippled through every aspect of Zappos' operations. Training programs, performance evaluations, hiring criteria – everything had to be reimagined once the fundamental assumption about what constituted good service was challenged.

Reverse Status Quo

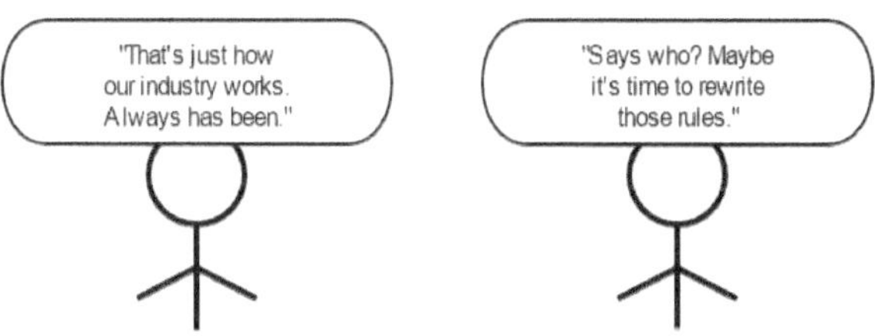

The Practice of Reverse Status Quo

The development and application of this mindset involves three fundamental practices, each requiring systematic cultivation and conscious application.

Assumption Archaeology

The first practice involves systematically uncovering and examining the hidden assumptions that shape industry behavior. This isn't just about listing obvious premises; it's about digging deep into the historical origins and unstated beliefs that guide current practices.

This requires careful study of how industry practices evolved, what historical conditions shaped them, and whether these conditions still apply. Often, practices that made sense decades ago persist long after their original rationale has disappeared. By understanding these historical roots, vacuum creators can identify which assumptions are truly foundational and which are merely historical artifacts.

Constraint Reframing

The second practice involves the systematic transformation of apparent limitations into sources of advantage. This requires developing the ability to see constraints not as fixed boundaries but as creative opportunities.

This practice begins with careful analysis of what makes something a constraint. Is it truly a physical limitation, or just a matter of perspective? Often, what appears to be a fundamental constraint is actually just a widely shared assumption about what's possible or practical.

Alternative Universe Building

The third practice involves actively designing and testing new systems freed from traditional constraints. This isn't just thought experiments; it's about creating concrete models of how things could work differently.

This requires developing the ability to envision and prototype completely new ways of operating. It involves creating small-scale experiments that can validate new approaches before scaling them, and building proof-of-concept models that demonstrate the viability of alternative paradigms.

Impact on Vacuum Creation

The power of reverse status quo thinking in vacuum creation manifests in three crucial ways:

First, it enables the discovery of entirely new solution spaces. By questioning basic assumptions, vacuum creators can identify opportunities that others literally cannot see because they're blocked by their acceptance of current constraints.

Second, it creates powerful competitive advantages. When you fundamentally rethink how something could work, you create positions that competitors find difficult to replicate – not because they lack the capability, but because they're still operating under old assumptions.

Finally, it enables natural market leadership. By being the first to imagine and implement new paradigms, reverse status quo thinkers often establish themselves as definitive leaders in newly created market spaces.

The reverse status quo mindset thus becomes not just a way of thinking but a systematic approach to identifying and creating new market opportunities. It enables vacuum creators to see possibilities where others see only constraints, and to turn industry limitations into sources of competitive advantage.

Mindset 5: Trust Orchestration

In the marketplace of human interaction, great vacuum creators see trust not as something that simply emerges over time, but as something to be carefully orchestrated from day one. While others wait for trust to develop naturally, they approach it with the same systematic thinking they apply to product development or market entry strategy.

Understanding Trust Orchestration

This mindset manifests in three key dimensions, each revealing a different aspect of how great vacuum creators systematically build trust.

1. Strategic Trust Cultivation

Consider Ratan Tata's approach across the Tata Group's diverse enterprises. While most large conglomerates saw corporate reputation as a marketing exercise, Tata envisioned trust as the fundamental currency of business relationships. In Tata Steel, this manifested through pioneering labor welfare practices, including one of India's first worker healthcare systems and pension schemes long before they were legally mandated. Tata Motors developed transparent pricing and comprehensive warranty systems that prioritized customer confidence over immediate financial gains.

This wasn't just about corporate social responsibility. Tata systematically built trust into every aspect of the group's operations. Tata Consultancy Services (TCS) implemented stringent data protection protocols and ethical AI practices before global regulations demanded them. Tata Chemicals developed sustainability initiatives that went beyond environmental compliance, actively restoring ecosystems where they operated. The group's telecommunications venture, Tata Teleservices, created customer communication channels that were unusually transparent about service limitations and pricing.

The genius lay in recognizing that trust wasn't just about maintaining a good image; it was about creating a new standard for how businesses could operate with integrity and social purpose. This systematic approach to trust-building became the foundation that helped establish the Tata Group as one of India's most respected and enduring business institutions, demonstrating that principled business practices could be both ethical and commercially successful.

2. Transparency as Innovation

Satya Nadella's transformation of Microsoft exemplifies this dimension. When he took over as CEO, Microsoft was known for its combative relationship with competitors and opacity around product development. Nadella saw an opportunity to turn radical transparency into a competitive advantage.

By making Microsoft's development processes more open, embracing open-source software, and publicly sharing the company's AI ethics principles, he transformed the company's relationship with developers, customers, and even competitors. This wasn't just PR – it was a fundamental reimagining of how a technology company could operate in the modern world.

The breakthrough came in recognizing that transparency could be a source of strength rather than vulnerability. By making the company's decision-making processes more visible and engaging with critics openly, Microsoft built deeper trust with its stakeholders and created a model for responsible technology leadership.

3. Trust as Compounding Asset

Daniel Zhang's work at Alibaba demonstrates the most sophisticated application of trust as a compounding asset. In a market where counterfeit goods and fraudulent sellers were common, Zhang didn't just implement better security measures – he created an entire ecosystem where trust could compound over time.

The innovation lay in treating trust not as a protective measure but as a growth engine. Each transaction, review, and interaction became part of a larger trust-building system. Sellers who maintained high trust scores gained better visibility. Buyers who provided reliable reviews earned higher credibility. The system created self-reinforcing cycles where good behavior was rewarded with increased opportunity.

Trust Orchestration

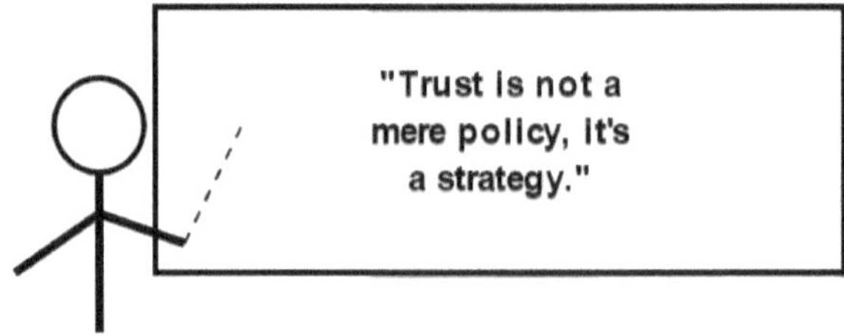

The Practice of Trust Orchestration

The development and application of this mindset involves three fundamental practices that transform how we think about building trust.

Strategic Trust Thinking

The first practice involves viewing trust not as a defensive measure but as an offensive strategy. Netflix's approach to content recommendations demonstrates this perfectly. Instead of hiding their algorithm's workings, they made their reasoning transparent, helping users understand why certain shows were recommended and building confidence in the system's suggestions.

This requires developing frameworks for:

- Identifying critical trust points in customer journeys

- Creating measurable trust objectives

- Building systems that demonstrate trustworthiness proactively

Transparency as a Strategy

Microsoft's transformation under Nadella shows how transparency can become a powerful strategic tool. This isn't about indiscriminate openness but about strategic transparency that builds competitive advantage.

The practice involves:

- Identifying areas where transparency creates value

- Designing systems that make complexity understandable

- Creating frameworks for responsible disclosure

Trust Multiplication

Alibaba's trust system demonstrates how to create self-reinforcing cycles of trust. This involves designing systems where trust builds upon itself, creating expanding networks of confidence.

Key elements include:

- Building trust transfer mechanisms between different parts of the ecosystem

- Creating incentives for trust-building behavior

- Developing systems where trust generates new opportunities

Impact on Vacuum Creation

Trust orchestration enables vacuum creation in three powerful ways:

First, it opens previously inaccessible markets. Netflix's trust-based approach helped create the streaming market when most thought digital distribution of premium content was impossible.

Second, it creates powerful competitive insulation. Microsoft's transformation through transparency built deeper stakeholder relationships that competitors find hard to replicate.

Third, it transforms trust from a cost center into a value driver. Alibaba's trust system didn't just reduce fraud – it created new business opportunities and market expansion possibilities.

The Trust Orchestration Mindset thus becomes not just a way of thinking about security or customer relationships, but a fundamental approach to creating and capturing new market opportunities. It enables vacuum creators to build sustainable advantages in markets where trust is a critical success factor.

Mindset 6: Scale Paradox Mastery

The rarest skill in business isn't achieving scale or maintaining customer intimacy – it's doing both simultaneously. The greatest vacuum creators possess an almost supernatural ability to think microscopically and astronomically at the same time.

This paradoxical ability – to maintain customer intimacy while achieving massive scale – represents perhaps the most sophisticated mindset of vacuum creation. While most business leaders see scale and personalization as opposing forces, the masters of vacuum creation understand how to make them mutually reinforcing.

Understanding Scale Paradox Mastery

This mindset manifests in three distinct dimensions, each revealing a different aspect of how great vacuum creators balance the seemingly unbalanceable.

1. **Intimate Mass Customization**

    Consider Netflix's approach to content personalization. While traditional media companies chose between broad appeal and niche focus, Netflix engineered a system that could simultaneously serve millions of viewers while making each feel like the service was personally curated for them.

    This wasn't just about sophisticated algorithms. Reed Hastings and his team created an entirely new paradigm for entertainment delivery. The same platform that could launch global phenomena like "Stranger Things" could also serve hyper-specialized content to tiny audience segments. Each viewer's homepage became a uniquely personalized theater, even as the platform scaled to hundreds of millions of subscribers.

The genius lay in recognizing that scale could actually enhance rather than diminish personalization. The more users joined the platform, the more data became available to refine recommendations, making each individual's experience more personal, not less. This systematic approach to using scale to drive intimacy became the foundation for a new kind of entertainment experience.

2. Infrastructure Intimacy

Jeff Bezos's work at Amazon exemplifies this dimension most powerfully. When others saw e-commerce scale as necessarily impersonal, he created systems that maintained individual attention even while serving hundreds of millions of customers. His insight was that technology, properly designed, could make massive operations feel intimate.

This wasn't just about personalized recommendations. Amazon built an entire infrastructure where scale and intimacy reinforced each other. The same systems that processed millions of orders could track individual customer preferences across years of purchases. The massive fulfillment networks could remember personal delivery preferences down to the individual doorstep.

Most remarkably, Bezos engineered systems where increased scale actually improved individual customer experience. The larger Amazon grew, the more data it had to personalize recommendations, the more efficient its delivery became, and the better it could predict individual customer needs.

3. Scalable Personalization

Howard Schultz's transformation of Starbucks demonstrates perhaps the most sophisticated application of scalable personalization. While others saw chain operations as necessarily standardized, Schultz created a system where each store, whether one of thousands, could maintain local character while leveraging global scale.

The breakthrough came in recognizing that standardization and personalization weren't opposites but complements. The same operational systems that ensured consistent quality could also enable baristas to remember individual customer preferences. Global supply chains could support local product variations. Standard training could empower personal connections.

Scale Paradox

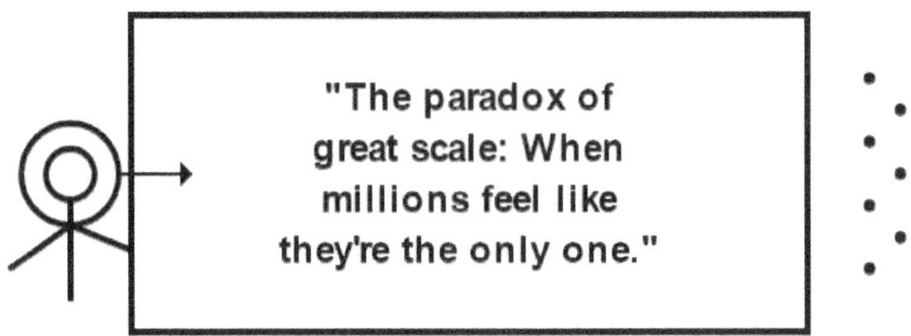

The Practice of Scale Paradox Mastery

The development and application of this mindset involves three fundamental practices that transform how we think about growth and intimacy.

Scale Architecture

The first practice involves designing systems where increased scale enhances rather than diminishes personal experience. Netflix's recommendation engine exemplifies this: the more users engage with the platform, the more personalized each individual's experience becomes.

This requires developing frameworks for:

- Creating feedback loops that improve with volume

- Building systems that learn from aggregate behavior to enhance individual experience

- Designing infrastructure that becomes more efficient and personal as it grows

Intimacy Engineering

The second practice involves systematically creating personal touchpoints within massive systems. Amazon's approach to customer service demonstrates this: even with hundreds of millions of customers, each interaction feels personal and informed by the customer's history.

Key elements include:

- Developing technologies that enable personal recognition at scale

- Creating systems that maintain context across multiple interactions

- Building frameworks for consistent yet personalized experiences

Paradox Integration

The third practice involves actively designing systems where scale and intimacy reinforce each other. Starbucks' store model shows how standardization can actually enable personalization when properly designed.

This requires:

- Creating platforms that become more personal as they grow

- Building systems where individual attention improves collective experience

- Developing frameworks where standardization enables customization

Impact on Vacuum Creation

Scale paradox mastery enables vacuum creation in three powerful ways:

First, it opens entirely new market segments. When you can maintain intimacy at scale, you can serve both mass markets and niche audiences simultaneously, creating opportunities that others see as mutually exclusive.

Second, it creates powerful competitive advantages. The ability to be both big and small – to leverage massive scale while maintaining personal touch – creates positions that competitors struggle to replicate. This isn't just about size or efficiency; it's about building systems that become more rather than less personal as they grow.

Third, it transforms growth from liability to asset. While traditional businesses often become more impersonal as they scale, masters of the scale paradox create systems where growth actually enhances individual experience. This turns what others see as a trade-off into a reinforcing cycle.

The Scale Paradox Mindset thus becomes not just a way of thinking about growth, but a fundamental approach to creating sustainable competitive advantages. It enables vacuum creators to build positions that others see as impossibly contradictory, turning apparent paradox into market opportunity.

Mindset 7: Legacy Consciousness

True vacuum creators don't build for the present; they architect for posterity. Their unique temporal perspective shapes not just what they build, but how their creations will be remembered and built upon by future generations. While most business leaders optimize quarterly results or even yearly performance, the masters of vacuum creation think in terms of decades and generations.

Understanding Legacy Consciousness

This mindset manifests in three key dimensions, each revealing a different aspect of how great vacuum creators build for the future.

1. **Generational Value Engineering**

   Consider Walt Disney's approach to entertainment legacy. While his contemporaries focused on producing hit movies or running successful studios, Disney was engineering an entire ecosystem of entertainment that would span generations. He wasn't just creating cartoons; he was building a system that would continue generating magic long after he was gone.

This wasn't just about creating enduring characters or stories. Disney systematically built institutions designed to outlast him: theme parks that would continue evolving, an animation studio with techniques that could be taught and refined, and a corporate culture centered on "imagineering." His innovation wasn't just in what he created, but in how he ensured it could keep creating.

The genius lay in understanding that true legacy isn't about preserving the past but enabling the future. Each element Disney created – from Mickey Mouse to Disneyland – was designed not just as a finished product but as a platform for future innovation. His systematic approach to legacy building became the foundation for what would become global entertainment's most enduring institution.

2. Future-Back Planning

Steve Jobs' second tenure at Apple exemplifies this dimension most powerfully. When he returned to Apple in 1997, Jobs didn't just focus on immediate survival or even medium-term success. He initiated a complete reimagining of consumer technology that would play out over decades.

This wasn't just strategic planning. Jobs systematically built capabilities and platforms that would enable future innovations he couldn't yet fully envision. The development of the Apple Store wasn't just about selling computers – it was about creating a physical presence that would support products that didn't yet exist. The switch to Intel processors wasn't just about performance – it was about creating an architecture that could evolve over decades.

Most remarkably, Jobs designed systems that would continue innovating even without his presence. He created not just products but ways of thinking about products that would guide Apple long after his departure. The company's ability to continue launching revolutionary products after his death testifies to the power of his future-back planning.

3. Values Architecture

Bill Gates' transformation from software tycoon to global philanthropist demonstrates perhaps the most sophisticated application of values architecture. While others focused on charitable giving, Gates engineered systems and institutions designed to solve generational problems.

The brilliance of his approach lay in creating frameworks that could evolve and adapt while maintaining core principles. The Bill & Melinda Gates Foundation wasn't designed just to distribute wealth but to systematically address global challenges across generations. Each initiative was structured not as a one-time intervention but as a catalyst for sustained change.

Legacy Consciousness

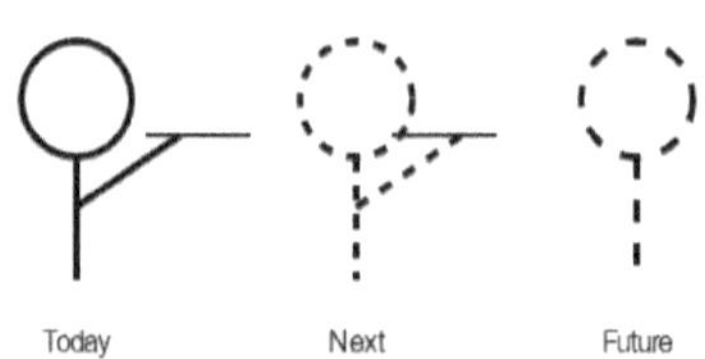

The Practice of Legacy Consciousness

The development of this mindset involves three fundamental practices that transform how we think about long-term impact.

Legacy Design

The first practice involves systematically creating systems that can outlive their creators. Disney's approach to animation demonstrates this perfectly: he didn't just create films; he created ways of creating films that could be taught, refined, and reinvented by future generations.

This requires developing frameworks for:

- Building institutions that can evolve while maintaining core values

- Creating systems that become stronger through succession

- Designing platforms that enable future innovation

Future Impact Mapping

The second practice involves actively designing for influence that compounds over time. Jobs' product architecture at Apple shows how this works: each innovation was designed not just as a product but as a platform that would enable future innovations.

Key elements include:

- Creating systems that generate new opportunities over time

- Building capabilities that appreciate rather than depreciate

- Developing frameworks that become more valuable as they mature

Value Transmission

The third practice involves creating mechanisms that ensure core principles and capabilities transfer effectively across generations. Gates' philanthropic work demonstrates this through:

- Systematic codification of learning and best practices

- Creation of institutional knowledge systems

- Development of principle-based decision frameworks

Impact on Vacuum Creation

Legacy consciousness enables vacuum creation in three powerful ways:

First, it creates sustainable innovation engines. By building systems designed to outlast their creators, legacy-conscious leaders create permanent sources of competitive advantage. Disney's animation studio continues generating new magic decades after its founder's passing.

Second, it builds compounding cultural capital. Strong values architecture creates organizational capabilities that strengthen over time. Apple's design philosophy continues evolving while maintaining its essential character.

Third, it transforms temporary success into lasting influence. By thinking in generational terms, legacy-conscious leaders create impacts that grow rather than diminish over time. Gates' philanthropic work continues expanding its influence through systematic design.

The Power of Legacy Thinking

In a world obsessed with immediate results, legacy consciousness provides a crucial competitive advantage. It enables vacuum creators to build not just successful enterprises but enduring institutions that continue generating value across generations.

The Symphony of Seven Mindsets

When I first discovered these mindsets, I realized something surprising: they're not about having extraordinary talent. They're about learning to look at the world through different lenses. It's like that moment when you put on a pair of glasses and suddenly everything snaps into focus – you see possibilities that were always there but just out of view.

What excites me most is how these mindsets work together. I think of them as instruments in an orchestra, each playing its own vital part in a larger symphony of innovation.

Here's how they harmonize:

- Through Intersectional Curiosity, you'll spot connections others miss

- With Temporal Arbitrage, you'll sense when an idea's time has come

- Using Systemic Simplification, you'll transform complex problems into elegant solutions

- By embracing Reverse Status Quo, you'll question what others take for granted

- Through Trust Orchestration, you'll build the foundations for lasting relationships

- With Scale Paradox Mastery, you'll maintain intimacy even as impact grows

- And Legacy Consciousness guides you to create enduring value

What I've found most empowering is that anyone can develop these mindsets. You don't need to be born with them – you just need the curiosity to explore, the courage to challenge assumptions, and the persistence to keep practicing. As our world grows more complex and fast-paced, these different ways of seeing become invaluable tools for spotting opportunities and creating meaningful change.

I've seen how mastering these mindsets can transform not just how we do business, but how we approach every challenge and opportunity. They're about more than success – they're about seeing the world's possibilities more clearly and doing something meaningful with what we see.

Parting Insight: Seeing the Invisible

As I reflect on the years of research that led to "The Vacuum Principle," one truth stands out: the most profound market opportunities often hide in plain sight. They're the empty spaces between what exists and what could be, waiting for someone with the right perspective to bring them to life.

Throughout this exploration of market vacuums, we've uncovered three fundamental truths:

First, market vacuums come in different forms – from feature and experience gaps to price, access, and trust opportunities. Like a naturalist learning to spot patterns in nature, successful innovators develop the ability to recognize these different types of opportunity spaces.

Second, filling these vacuums isn't about luck or intuition. It requires systematic frameworks for spotting opportunities, engineering solutions, and timing market entry. The most successful market creators combine rigorous analysis with creative insight.

Third, and perhaps most importantly, the ability to see and fill market vacuums isn't a gift bestowed upon a chosen few. It's a capability that can be developed through the seven mindsets we've explored – from intersectional curiosity to legacy consciousness. This is the essence of The Vacuum Principle: learning to see and seize the opportunities that exist in empty spaces.

I'm often asked what separates great market creators from everyone else. The answer isn't superior resources or even better ideas. It's their ability to see what others overlook – the gaps between what is and what could be. They develop what I call "vacuum vision" – the ability to spot opportunities in empty spaces where others see nothing at all.

As you close this book and begin applying these principles, remember that every transformative innovation began with someone seeing a space that others missed. The markets of tomorrow are shaped by those who can master The Vacuum Principle – those who learn to spot and fill the vacuums of today.

The spaces are there, waiting to be filled. The only question is: what will you create in them?

References and Citations

Natural vs. Created Vacuums

A. Books

1. Christensen, C. M. (1997). The Innovator's Dilemma. Harvard Business Review Press.

2. Levy, S. (2010). In the Plex: How Google Thinks, Works, and Shapes Our Lives. Simon & Schuster.

3. Isaacson, W. (2011). Steve Jobs. Simon & Schuster.

B. Academic Papers

1. Henderson, R. M., & Clark, K. B. (1990). Architectural Innovation: The Reconfiguration of Existing Product Technologies and the Failure of Established Firms. Administrative Science Quarterly, 35(1), 9-30.

2. Tushman, M. L., & Anderson, P. (1986). Technological Discontinuities and Organizational Environments. Administrative Science Quarterly, 31(3), 439-465.

C. Company Annual Reports

    1.   Tesla, Inc. Annual Reports (2010-2015)

    2.   Uber Technologies, Inc. Annual Reports and S-1 Filing

D. Journalistic Sources

    1.   Bilton, N. (2013). Hatching Twitter: A True Story of Money, Power, Friendship, and Betrayal. Portfolio.

    2.   Lashinsky, A. (2012). Inside Apple: How America's Most Admired--and Secretive--Company Really Works. Business Plus.

    3.   Wong, B. (2018). "How Uber's Early Days Shaped Its Culture". Wired Magazine.

References for: The Five Types of Market Vacuums

A. Books

    1.   Kim, W. C., & Mauborgne, R. (2005). Blue Ocean Strategy. Harvard Business School Press.

    2.   Ries, E. (2011). The Lean Startup. Crown Business.

    3.   Porter, M. E. (1980). Competitive Strategy. Free Press.

B. Academic Papers

    1.   Prahalad, C. K., & Hamel, G. (1990). The Core Competence of the Corporation. Harvard Business Review, 68(3), 79-91.

    2.   Christensen, C. M. (1997). Disruptive Innovation Theory. Harvard Business Review.

C. Company Annual Reports

1. Apple Inc. Annual Reports (2007-2015)

2. Amazon.com, Inc. Annual Reports (2010-2018)

D. Journalistic Sources

1. Levy, S. (2011). In the Plex: How Google Thinks, Works, and Shapes Our Lives. Simon & Schuster.

2. Stone, B. (2013). The Everything Store: Jeff Bezos and the Age of Amazon. Little, Brown and Company.

References for: Vacuum Spotting

A. Books

1. Christensen, C. M. (1997). The Innovator's Dilemma. Harvard Business Review Press.

2. Thiel, P. (2014). Zero to One: Notes on Startups, or How to Build the Future. Crown Business.

3. Ries, E. (2011). The Lean Startup. Crown Business.

B. Academic Papers

1. Drucker, P. F. (1985). Innovation and Entrepreneurship. Harvard Business Review.

2. Teece, D. J. (2007). Explicating Dynamic Capabilities: The Nature and Microfoundations of (Sustainable) Enterprise Performance. Strategic Management Journal, 28(13), 1319-1350.

C. Company Annual Reports

1. Southwest Airlines Annual Reports (1970-2000)

2. Netflix, Inc. Annual Reports (2000-2010)

D. Journalistic Sources

1. Gladwell, M. (2000). The Tipping Point: How Little Things Can Make a Big Difference. Little, Brown and Company.

2. Isaacson, W. (2011). Steve Jobs. Simon & Schuster.

3. Lewis, M. (2014). Flash Boys: A Wall Street Revolt. W. W. Norton & Company.

References for: Vacuum Engineering

A. Books

1. Christensen, C. M. (2003). The Innovator's Solution. Harvard Business Review Press.

2. Collins, J. (2001). Good to Great. Harper Business.

3. Kawasaki, G. (2011). Enchantment: The Art of Changing Hearts, Minds, and Actions. Portfolio.

B. Academic Papers

1. Teece, D. J. (2010). Business Models, Business Strategy and Innovation. Long Range Planning, 43(2-3), 172-194.

2. Chesbrough, H. (2010). Business Model Innovation: Opportunities and Barriers. Long Range Planning, 43(2-3), 354-363.

C. Company Annual Reports

1. McDonald's Corporation Annual Reports (1955-2000)

2. Tesla, Inc. Annual Reports (2010-2020)

D. Journalistic Sources

1. Keough, D. (2008). The Ten Principles for Building a Great Enterprise. Currency.

2. Lashinsky, A. (2012). Inside Apple: How America's Most Admired--and Secretive--Company Really Works. Business Plus.

3. Buford, K. (2012). The Founder's Dilemmas: Anticipating and Avoiding the Pitfalls That Can Sink a Startup. Princeton University Press.

References: Vacuum Timing

A. Books

1. Clayton, C. M. (1997). The Innovator's Dilemma. Harvard Business Review Press.

2. Taleb, N. N. (2007). The Black Swan: The Impact of the Highly Improbable. Random House.

3. Hoffman, R., & Yeh, C. (2018). Blitzscaling: The Lightning-Fast Path to Building Massively Valuable Companies. Currency.

B. Academic Papers

1. Utterback, J. M., & Abernathy, W. J. (1975). A Dynamic Model of Process and Product Innovation. Omega, 3(6), 639-656.

2. Rogers, E. M. (1962). Diffusion of Innovations. Free Press.

C. Company Annual Reports

1. Amazon.com, Inc. Annual Reports (2000-2010)

2. Netflix, Inc. Annual Reports (2007-2015)

3. Spotify AB Annual Reports (2010-2020)

D. Journalistic Sources

1. Isaacson, W. (2011). Steve Jobs. Simon & Schuster.

2. Stone, B. (2013). The Everything Store: Jeff Bezos and the Age of Amazon. Little, Brown and Company.

3. Levy, S. (2011). In the Plex: How Google Thinks, Works, and Shapes Our Lives. Simon & Schuster.

References: Protecting & Scaling Vacuums

A. Books

1. Porter, M. E. (1985). Competitive Advantage. Free Press.

2. Collins, J. (2001). Good to Great. Harper Business.

3. Christensen, C. M. (2003). The Innovator's Solution. Harvard Business Review Press.

B. Academic Papers

1. Teece, D. J. (2007). Dynamic Capabilities and Strategic Management. Strategic Management Journal, 28(13), 1319-1350.

2. Prahalad, C. K., & Hamel, G. (1990). The Core Competence of the Corporation. Harvard Business Review, 68(3), 79-91.

C. Company Annual Reports

1. Shopify Inc. Annual Reports (2015-2023)

2. Apple Inc. Annual Reports (2010-2020)

D. Journalistic Sources

1. Stone, B. (2013). The Everything Store: Jeff Bezos and the Age of Amazon. Little, Brown and Company.

2. Levy, S. (2011). In the Plex: How Google Thinks, Works, and Shapes Our Lives. Simon & Schuster.

3. Lashinsky, A. (2012). Inside Apple: How America's Most Admired--and Secretive--Company Really Works. Business Plus.

About the Author

Rajesh Srinivasan is a business strategy and modern marketing expert with a deep philosophical inquiry into the patterns that shape industries, human behavior, culture, and consciousness. As a consultant and keynote speaker, he brings a unique blend of practical expertise and intellectual curiosity.

An accomplished author of four books, Rajesh's latest work, *Mindful Marketing*, a distinctive cartoon-based book, became a bestseller on Amazon. Beyond writing and speaking, he is a trusted advisor to entrepreneurs, CEOs, and CXOs, providing strategic insights into business, marketing, and brand strategy development.

Widely respected in the industry, Rajesh is a sought-after keynote speaker, regularly delivering impactful masterclasses at industry forums and corporate annual planning meetings.

Outside of his professional life, Rajesh is a dedicated mindfulness practitioner and enjoys connecting with nature. He cherishes personal time, often spending it with his wife Priya and son Vishal, balancing intellectual pursuits with family warmth.

www.rajeshsrinivasan.com